THE GOLDEN ISLES OF GEORGIA

FANNY KEMBLE AS "BIANCA"
(A Portrait Painted by Thomas Sully)

THE GOLDEN ISLES
OF GEORGIA

By

CAROLINE COUPER LOVELL

With Illustrations

CHEROKEE PUBLISHING COMPANY
Atlanta, Georgia

This book is printed on acid-free paper which conforms to the American National Standard Z39.48-1984 *Permanence of Paper for Printed Library Materials.* Paper that conforms to this standard's requirements for pH, alkaline reserve and freedom from groundwood is anticipated to last several hundred years without significant deterioration under normal library use and storage conditions.

Cover photo by Carroll Proctor Scruggs

Manufactured in the United States of America

ISBN: 973-0-87797-012-5 Hardcover
ISBN: 973-0-87797-316-4 Paper

Originally published 1932

 Cherokee Publishing Company
P O Box 1730, Marietta, GA 30061

Dedicated to the memory of
CHARLES SPALDING WYLLY
Captain 1st Georgia Regulars, C. S. A.

THE AUTHOR

Caroline Couper Lovell, author of *The Golden Isles of Georgia*, was born at "Etowah Cliffs," the home of her paternal grandfather in Bartow County, Georgia, in 1862. She was the daughter of Robert Mackay Stiles and the former Margaret Wylly Couper. Through her mother she was descended from the Wylly and Couper families which had distinguished themselves early in Georgia's history.

Young Miss Stiles was educated by a governess and at Madame LeFevre's fashionable school for girls in Baltimore. In an 1884 ceremony at "Malbone," a house which her parents had built close to "Etowah Cliffs," she became the bride of William Storrow Lovell. He was a native of Mississippi whose early years had been divided between his parents' homes in New Orleans, on Palmyra Island in the Mississippi River, and at Sewanee, Tennessee.

Soon after her marriage Mrs. Lovell studied art during a lengthy sojourn in Paris, after which she and her husband spent nearly four years on their Palmyra Island plantation. They moved to Birmingham in 1888 and soon became leading figures in the city's social and cultural life. After more than fifty years of marriage, Mr. Lovell died and his widow returned to her native Georgia. She settled at Savannah, where she lived happily and tranquilly until her death in 1947. Both Mr. and Mrs. Lovell, who were childless, are buried in Birmingham.

The Golden Isles of Georgia was written by Mrs. Lovell over a period of six or so years prior to its publication in 1932. She based it largely upon the "Memoirs" of her uncle, Charles Spalding Wylly, a Confederate veteran from Darien who died at Brunswick in 1923. This charming story made an immediate hit with lovers of Georgia's historic and romantic coastal area. Long out of print, it is now made available to a new generation of readers as the seventh title in Cherokee Publishing Company's reprint series of rare items of Georgiana.

—*William Bailey Williford*

FOREWORD

CHARLES SPALDING WYLLY of Darien, Georgia, spent the last years of his long life in Brunswick. Sharing the fate of the old, he found it almost impossible to get work, though still strong in body and mind. To divert and interest him, his niece, Mrs. William S. Lovell, suggested that he write his memoirs. He wrote *Memories, The Annals of Glynn,* and *The Seed That Was Sown,* which were published through the liberality of his friend, Columbia Downing of Brunswick.

The manuscripts of the first two little books were presented to his niece, with other unpublished data.

After Captain Wylly's death in 1923, as there had been no second edition of these works, it was suggested that Mrs. Lovell should edit them. This she attempted to do, and then decided that it would be better to use the material, add to it, and compile another story. The result is *The Golden Isles of Georgia,* much of which has been freely quoted from Captain Wylly's writings.

She was also granted the privilege of using the

Memoirs of Mrs. Holmes Conrad, by Mrs. Conrad's daughters, and of Mrs. George C. Dent, by her granddaughter, Miss Miriam Dent, of Hofwyl, Georgia.   Private papers and letters of the Pages and Kings were lent by Mrs. Randolph Anderson of Savannah, and information in regard to the Gould and Cater families was supplied by Mrs. Agnes C. Hartridge and Mrs. William H. Shadman of St. Simon's.

CONTENTS

ILLUSTRATIONS

THE GOLDEN ISLES OF GEORGIA

I

GUALE

ALONG the arc of the Georgia coast, from the mouth of the Savannah River to that of the St. Mary's, there is a chain of sea islands. On their eastern shores the white surf of the Atlantic rolls ceaselessly, and behind them lie the still waters of inland channels, stretches of quiet marsh, and the mainland.

Two great rivers flow into the sounds between these islands—the Ogeechee, not far from the Savannah, and the Altamaha, a little more than halfway down the coast. The Altamaha, the nobler stream, is formed by the junction of the Ocmulgee and the Oconee, which rise in northern Georgia. A broad and beautiful river as it nears the sea, its banks are bordered by a dense growth of live oak and cypress, magnolia and bay, all swathed in a tangled cobweb of floating gray moss; and on either bank, beyond the tropical growth of the stream, endless pine forests rise from a thick undergrowth of scrub palmetto.

The islands are as densely wooded as the banks of the Altamaha, though here and there in the interiors are open savannas, covered with harsh wire grass, where palmetto trees stand, clean cut against the burning blue of the Southern sky.   And where the land is low there are swamps, in which the spreading knees of the cypress are like Indian tepees, reflected in the wine-dark water.   The woods are filled with the fragrance of myrtle, bay, and jessamine, and the only sounds that break the stillness are the musical notes of birds and the murmur of the wind-surf in the pines.

The soil of these islands is fertile, and in the early days the Indian women who lived on them cultivated small patches of corn, beans, and pumpkins, while their men hunted and fished.   These Indians seem to have been docile and peaceably inclined, and offered no resistance when the Spaniards attempted to civilize them.

Following the conquest of Florida, Spain claimed the Atlantic Coast, by right of discovery and occupation, as far north as the mouth of the James.   In 1526, a short-lived colony was established on the Carolina coast, other expeditions followed, and in 1540 De Soto's imposing cavalcade of mounted cavaliers traversed southern Georgia on its way to the Mississippi in its hopeless quest for gold.

When, in 1562, the French sent over two fleets
to establish Huguenot colonies on the Southern
coast, Spain challenged the right of France to settle
in her realm. Charlefort, which they built on
Port Royal Sound, had to be abandoned within the
year, while Fort Caroline, near the St. John's, was
destroyed, and its garrison mercilessly massacred.
In 1565, San Augustin was founded by Menéndez de Avilés, *adelantado* and captain-general of
Florida, and within the year a line of posts was established as far north as Santa Elena, which the
Spaniards had named many years before. San
Augustin, the oldest city in the United States, was
an ecclesiastical offshoot of the diocese of Santiago
de Cuba. Both Church and State were anxious to
extend the dominion of Spanish power, and with it
the spread of Catholicism. Philip II of Spain had
learned from the futile Spanish expeditions that
the Atlantic Coast offered no wealth of gold or silver, but he thought it expedient to plant his flag
in this unknown country and to raise the cross beside it. And so it came about that, as early as 1568,
missions were established on the islands of the
Georgia coast, and the conversion of the Indians
began.

North from San Augustin, the first of the seven
large coast islands, now known as Cumberland,

was called by the Spaniards San Pedro, its Indian name having been Missoe, which is said to mean sassafras. Next comes Jekyl, which retained its Indian name of Ospo. St. Simon's, north of this, which had been Asao, they called San Simon. Sapelo was named Zápala after a province in Spain. St. Catherine's Island was known as Santa Catalina, and also as Guale. Ossabaw was the Indian Obispa, and either Skidaway or Tybee, Chatuachee. Santa Catalina was visited the year after the founding of San Augustin by the great Menéndez, who was hospitably received by an old Indian named Guale, after whom the island was called. Because of its importance later on as ecclesiastical headquarters, the whole district was called Guale.

Santa Catalina was first settled by a band of thirty Spaniards, soon followed by a hundred and fifty others, who established themselves on San Pedro, San Simon, and Zápala.

Menéndez was known as the Great White Father, and his rule was enforced from Tampa Bay to Norfolk Harbor. At San Augustin and Santa Elena he established *presidios,* where he placed colonists, with soldiers to defend them, and between the two he erected outposts to guard the inland passages and islands. The most important of these were at

Tolomato, on the mainland opposite Zápala, and at
Tupiqui, three leagues inland.

The first laborers in the vineyard of the Lord
were Jesuits, and their work was baptized in blood,
for no sooner had Father Martinez stepped on the
soil of Guale than he was brutally slain by a Timu-
cua native, who killed him with a wooden axe or
macana. But his martyrdom only inspired other
Jesuits to hasten across the sea. Among those
who came were Brothers Domingo Augustin and
Pedro Ruiz. On Santa Catalina they learned the
Guale language, and in six months had translated
the catechism and written a grammar, besides visiting and teaching on all of the islands. The north-
ernmost of these was Oristo, now the island of
Edisto, in South Carolina, where Father Rogel
had charge.

On all of the islands the Jesuits established missions and built chapels. Converts were gained,
usually by means of gifts, so-called schools were
started, and a semblance of worship brought about.
The Fathers were encouraged and hopeful, as the
work seemed promising and the Indians were willing to submit to their mild form of authority.
But before long hunger and disease caused discontent and strife, and in two years' time the Jesuits
were forced to abandon their mission of mercy.

For three years the Indians were left to themselves, perhaps happier in their ignorance, until, in 1573, the Little Brothers of Saint Francis accepted the call to Florida, and, coming over, took charge of the Guale Missions. The most ardent of these was Father Aloyso Reynoso, who journeyed from Santa Elena to all of the islands, and from thence to Spain, to raise funds and bring back other missionaries.

Travel among the islands was by way of the inland routes, large canoes, called periaguas, being rowed back and forth to carry the priests and settlers, and bring their supplies. These boats were usually hewn from cypress trees, which were sometimes split down the centre, and widened by means of boards. Occasionally the oars were supplemented by sails, and the periaguas were used even at sea, sailing up and down the Atlantic Coast. The brown-robed Fathers often paddled their own small dugouts when hastening to the bedside of sick or dying converts on the mainland, going in these as far as the Mission of Santo Domingo de Telage, up on the great Altamaha.

The Franciscans had probably many hardships to bear, but there were compensations. The climate of the islands was delightful, mild in winter and moderated in summer by cool breezes from the ocean, and it was a place of abundance. The native fishermen caught shrimps, crabs, and turtles, as well as a great variety of fish, and the hunters shot wild turkeys and deer, which they brought over to the islands and sold for a trifling sum. Figs, oranges, and pomegranates were planted and flourished, and the good Fathers must have felt that this land, contrasted with the cold and aridity of most of Spain, was an earthly Paradise.

The peaceful life of the islands was not undisturbed, however, for before long a French fleet anchored in the harbor of Gualquini, which lay between Ospo and San Simon. The French had come ostensibly to trade with the Indians for sassafras, wild turkeys, deer, and beaver skins. Wild turkeys were plentiful on the islands of Ospo, San Simon, and Zápala, and some of these, being sent to the King of France, were introduced into Europe a half century before the Puritans discovered them in New England. The French felt bitterly towards the Spaniards, and, plotting now with the Indians, they threw the whole district into disorder.

An even more serious disaster threatened the Missions when, in 1586, Sir Francis Drake, great English sea rover or pirate, burned San Augustin and spread consternation along the entire coast. The troops were brought down from Santa Elena, and the island of Santa Catalina became the northern outpost of the Spaniards. The danger passed, however, and by the end of the century the islands had prospered and become so important that eight new missionaries were assigned to the province. Plans were now made to extend the work of conversion into the interior. Two fearless pioneers, Fathers Chozas and Velascola, the Cantabrian giant, journeyed eight days on horseback to the Creek villages on the upper Altamaha, the Oconee, and the Ocmulgee. They were favorably received, stayed for some time, and made plans for the erection of mission outposts.

It was at this time, when their prospects were brightest, that disaster overtook the Franciscans. The two missionaries had just returned from the interior, Chozas to San Pedro and Velascola to San Simon, when an outbreak among the Indians brought about their destruction.

Juan, the heir of the Mico of Tolomato, incensed by the restraints imposed on him by Father Corpa of Obispa, led a band of Indians to his mission, and murdered him as he slept. This taste of blood aroused the ferocity of the natives, who swept from Catalina down to San Simon, sacking, burning, and destroying every Spanish settlement. Five priests and three laymen won the crown of martyrdom.

Father Rodriguez was slain at Tupiqui, Fathers Anton and Badajoz on Santa Catalina, the giant Velascola on San Simon, while Father Davila was wounded on Ospo and taken off into captivity. The island of San Pedro alone escaped, for, though attacked by a fleet of forty canoes, the resident natives remained faithful, and the arrival of a Spanish galley, which landed a hundred and fifty soldiers, brought aid and secured its safety. On this island a nucleus was preserved, from which the authorities reëstablished the ravaged missions and rebuilt the chapels which had been destroyed. A year later Father Davila was rescued, the island chiefs, renewing their allegiance, were pardoned, and by 1605 the missions of Guale were completely restored.

A year after, His Lordship, Bishop Calderon of Cuba, came up for the first Episcopal visitation ever made in this country. He visited the islands and the parish of Santa Maria on the St. Mary's River, and during his stay 1070 natives were confirmed.

It was probably during the seventeenth century, which is called the Golden Age of the Franciscans in the Old Southeast, that there were built the substantial churches and monasteries of which we are told. The material used for these buildings was coquina, or tabby, a mixture of crushed oyster shells and cement, poured into moulds and tamped down, which is said to be almost indestructible.

On each of the islands were a resident priest and one or more lay brothers, and on every island must have sounded the musical bells of the chapels, calling the faithful to prayer. On Santa Catalina, Bernardo de los Angeles was in charge. On Ossabaw, Pedro de Lastere, with two lay brothers, cared for their own mission, and for the outlying mission of Chatuachee. Jean Baptist de Campana had the mission of San Jose de Zápala; Juan de Useeda that of Santo Domingo at Telaje on the main; while Pedro de Luna, with one lay brother, was in charge of the mission of San Buenaventura on San Simon.

Although it was their Golden Age, these good and devoted priests still had much to contend with. More than once epidemics swept off a large part of the island population, and raids of hostile Indians carried off many of their converts. But they never lost heart, and in 1666 they celebrated the centennial of Guale.

The end, however, was in sight, for in 1670 the English established the settlement of Charleston, on what the Spaniards considered their land, and San Augustin prepared for war. A number of frigates sailed to Charleston Harbor, and the little settlement would undoubtedly have been destroyed but for a storm, which dispersed the fleet and saved the village. In the same year Spain and England came to terms, and a treaty was signed, the possession of Charleston being assured to England and that of all the coast south of it to Spain.

In spite of this treaty, aggression on the part of the English continued, and, realizing that it would only be a question of time before San Augustin was attacked, the Spaniards began to build a fort at that place, which is still in existence. Constructed of stone and tabby, it was strong enough to resist two sieges by the English later on. In addition to fortifying San Augustin, the Spaniards put the coast islands in as strong a state of defense as possible.

This was fortunate, as the expected invasion soon came, the Indian allies of the English being the first to attack the islands, striking at almost the same time at Santa Catalina, San Simon, and Ospo. Catalina stood an all-day siege, finally repulsing the enemy, but Ospo, the weakest of the islands, would have been destroyed had not Captain Fuentes come to its rescue.

The morale of the Gualians was weakened by this invasion, and the Spanish frontier now dropped down from Santa Catalina to Zápala, where it remained for six years. Here a substantial fort was built and commanded by Captain Fuentes, and for a time the islanders enjoyed again the blessings of peace. It was not for long, however, for pirates from the Caribbean began to raid them, carrying off stock and plunder and taking even the altar plate from the churches.

In 1685, the Carolina colonists, combining with the Creeks of Georgia and the Yemasee Indians, a warlike tribe whose wigwams bordered the Savannah River, declared war against the Spaniards and their allies, the converted Indians of the coast. The Spanish Government made every effort to persuade the Indians to leave the islands north of San Pedro, but they refused to heed their priests and, totally unprepared for resistance, were attacked by an overwhelming force. A great fleet of canoes, filled with hostile Indians, landed on Santa Catalina, and sacked and burned the mission and all other buildings. The natives fled to the woods, where they were pursued, the men butchered, and the women and children taken captive.

The same fate befell Obispa and Zápala, and on the mainland the English and their fierce allies crossed the Altamaha, and, going down as far as eighty-five miles west of San Augustin, destroyed an inland mission. They returned to Charleston with their spoils, and the wretched Indian captives were sold, and sent to Cuba and the West Indies as slaves.

Governor Cabrera of San Augustin rescued the few remaining natives from the islands of Guale, brought them down to Florida, and settled them within the zone of Spanish protection. A garrison was stationed at Santa Maria, which became, with the island of San Pedro, the final Spanish outpost on the north.

It was in this year, 1686, that Jonathan Dickenson made his memorable voyage in a canoe, from St. Mary's to Beaufort, South Carolina. In his *Journal of the Wonderful Deliverance*, published in London, he tells of having been wrecked on the Florida coast, of being forwarded by the Governor of San Augustin to the Mission at Mariana. The priests in charge there sent him on, in a canoe paddled by Indians, to Beaufort, which he reached in eight days, and he wrote of seeing the ruins of former missions on the islands as he passed. "The islands are abandoned and uninhabited," he wrote, "but show traces of having once been posts of great importance. More than 300 acres seem to have been in cultivation, and the ruins of many buildings are visible."

In a few years even these ruins disappeared, for in 1702 Governor Moore of South Carolina attempted to destroy San Augustin, sailing south by the inland passages with a fleet of galleys and peri-aguas. The fort was besieged for a month, when the siege was abandoned and the Governor returned by the same route to Charleston, leaving a trail of death and destruction in his wake.

The islands of the Georgia coast being now practically deserted, Edward Teach, the infamous pirate, known as Blackbeard, used them as places of refuge, and the island of Black Beard in Doboy Sound still bears his name. This villain, who was so called because of his bushy black beard, the ends of which he tied with ribbons around his ears, committed his crimes on the Spanish Main, among the West Indies, and along the Carolina coast, until captured in 1718 and executed.

By the time the Saxon race was established in Georgia in 1733, every vestige of the Spanish civilization which had flourished for over a hundred and twenty-five years had vanished from the islands of the coast. Every native convert of the Catholic Church had disappeared, the men having been slain or sold into slavery — the women sharing the same fate — or merged into other Indian tribes.

Of all the substantial buildings, forts, churches, and monasteries which the Spaniards erected, only one authentic ruin remains in existence. This is

situated six miles from St. Mary's and is undoubtedly the remains of the Mission of Santa Maria de
Guadeloupe, still known as Mariana. On the
plantation of Evelyn, near the Altamaha, in Glynn
County, there is another ruin which may have been
built by the Spaniards. All the old books mention
it, though no one has been able to connect it with
a known occupation.

Through the recent discovery of old Spanish ar-
chives, many of the tabby ruins on the Georgia
coast, and its islands, have been claimed to be the
ruins of Spanish edifices. If this is true, it is
strange that none of the oldest coast inhabitants
knew of any traditions to that effect.

Gone are the "Golden Isles of Guale" into an
almost mythical past. Over the ruins of its missions, erected two centuries before those of California, forests have grown. Stilled forever are
its musical bells, and only in the lovely names bestowed on the islands by the Spaniards is there a
memory of the days when they belonged to Spain.

Ossabaw — Obispa. St. Catherine's — Santa
Catalina. Sapelo — Zápala. St. Simon's — San
Simon.

II

NEW INVERNESS

WHEN Oglethorpe founded Savannah in 1733, the islands along the Georgia coast were uninhabited. Among the Creek Indians they were known as the Hunting Islands, and resorted to at certain seasons for hunting and fishing.

Spain still claimed the coast and islands of Georgia, and the Carolinas were in constant dread of an attack from Florida. Their runaway slaves found an asylum in St. Augustine, and, to prevent their escape, the English built a fort on the Altamaha. The Spaniards protested, and, when, soon after, the fort was burned, it was never rebuilt.

The British Government now realized that it was necessary to protect their Southern Colonies, and decided to establish a free colony — in which slavery would not be allowed — between South Carolina and Florida. When, about this time, the philanthropic plan of Oglethorpe and his associates was laid before it, it was readily adopted. To the unfortunate debtors and deserving poor, free passage was offered, lands granted, and a three-year support guaranteed. And thus it was that, brought about by political necessity, but born of the purest feelings that emanate from the human heart, the Colony of Georgia came into being.

South Carolina ceded her claims to the lands that now comprise the states of Georgia, Alabama, and Mississippi, and the youngest of the American Colonies was called Georgia, in honor of George II, King of Great Britain.

The site chosen for the city of Savannah was Yamacraw Bluff, eighteen miles from the mouth of the Savannah River, where land was obtained from Tomocheche, an aged Indian chief. As soon as the colonists were established, Oglethorpe invited the head men of the Creek nation to a conference.

In spite of the claims of Spain, the Creeks considered the Georgia coast their own, and they now made a friendly treaty with the English, granting them all of the coast land between the Savannah and the Altamaha Rivers, reserving for their own use only the hunting islands of Ossabaw, St. Catherine's, and Sapelo.

This encroachment on their realm naturally deepened the enmity of the Spaniards, and the Georgia Trustees now thought it prudent to establish a military outpost on the Altamaha. The poor, rescued from starvation in England, had turned out to be a wretched lot, idle and useless, and it was resolved that hereafter settlers should be restricted to those whose nativity and habits of life gave promise of thrift and industry. Courage was requisite above all for life on a dangerous frontier, and the mountains of Scotland were mentioned as "worthy of careful investigation."

The Jacobite rebellion, under the Earls of Mar and Argyle, had been suppressed in 1715. The lands of those who had rebelled had been forfeited, and their social standing lost. Many Northern gentlemen were homeless and penniless, and some were outlawed and in hiding. The Borlam McIntoshes, a younger branch of the McIntoshes of Moy, were deeply involved. The elder branch had remained seemingly loyal, and retained their possessions, while the younger found themselves under the ban. Thus the family, relatives, and dependents of Lachlan McIntosh of Borlam lent a willing ear when Lieutenant McKay came to Inverness with an offer of free transportation, free land, and a free life in a new country.

On October 18, 1735, the ship *Prince of Wales,* Captain Dunbar, sailed from the port of Inverness, carrying a hundred and thirty Highlanders with fifty women and children. Twelve were passengers paying their own way, and each of these was to be given a grant of five hundred acres in the new country. The largest number of Highlanders were from the Glen of Stralbdean, nine miles from Inverness, while their minister, the Reverend John McLeod, was a native of the Isle of Skye. They were commanded by their own chiefs, John Morh McIntosh being their leader. He had married Mary Mackay, and William, the eldest of their four sons, was at this time nine years of age. With the McIntoshes of Bain and Lynvulgie were the Mc-Bains of Clan Buie, the McDonalds, McKays, Cuthberts, Morrisons, Baillies, Dunbars, Wrights, and others. They were all picked men of honor, and every man was a soldier. A bold and hardy set, strong, fearless, and willing to work.

The *Prince of Wales* made Tybee Island in December, and the new colonists were at once sent south to the Altamaha. They were rowed down in periaguas along those inland waters where the Franciscan Fathers had paddled their dugouts in other days, and, coming from the mists and mountains of Scotland, the contrast must have been striking, for here they found a wide, flat world of sunshine, ever changing, ever lovely, peaceful and serene. On one hand woods of pine, oak, and cedar grew close to the waterside, while the sea-green, faintly rippled channel was bordered on the other by a world of yellow marsh, beyond which the sea islands were dreams of lilac against the sky.

Strange sounds came from the mysterious marsh — the strident notes of unseen birds, and now and then the clattering call of a marsh hen. Overhead sea gulls, startlingly white against the blue, sailed up from the sea, wheeled, and sailed back again.

Entering the broad mouth of the Altamaha, the colonists proceeded a few miles up the river to a high bluff on the north bank, where it had been decided to establish the town of New Inverness. The plateau was protected on the east by a creek, on the west by Cat River, and on it was a grove of majestic live oaks. Beneath these trees temporary huts were erected for the settlers, and over them the flag of England was unfurled. As soon as possible a fort was constructed, manned by four cannon, and a guardhouse, store, and chapel were built.

The men who were subject to military duty were mustered into the King's service as the Highland Rangers, and all males between the ages of sixteen and fifty-five were liable to the call of the post commander if necessary for the public defense. The immediate command of the Rangers fell, by right of birth and choice, to John Morh McIntosh, while the post of Commander was bestowed on Captain Hugh McKay, second son of Baron Reay of Scotland, and an officer in the royal army.

Ten miles above New Inverness, on the Altamaha, Fort Howe was established, commanding the fords of the great river. A patrol and scouting party kept up daily communication with this fort, while another connected it with Fort Argyle on the Ogeechee, where the Indian war trail crossed that river. From this fort there was a third patrol to Savannah. Below New Inverness, on the mainland, was the outpost of Carteret's.

The military posts being established, it was now decided to connect New Inverness directly with Savannah by a road running along the coast. This highway, which is known as Oglethorpe's Road, was the first ever constructed in Georgia, and is still in use. It is a beautiful white shell road running level through forests of moss-draped oaks and purple pines, fragrant in spring with the delicious odor of jessamine, magnolia, and bay; skirting dark swamps, then emerging into brilliant sunshine as it winds along spacious marshes beside the flowing and flooding tide.

For some time the Highlanders of New Inverness preserved their national garb, and, in a measure, their speech. When Oglethorpe made his first visit of inspection in the winter of 1736, he was received on the bluff by a force of fifty men, in full Highland costume "with claymore, plaid and target." This was the first parade of any regular Colonial military body in Georgia. Captain McIntosh offered the General the use of his house or hut, and a couch fitted with the only pair of sheets owned by the Scots, but Oglethorpe gallantly declined, and lay instead by the guard fire, wrapped in his plaid. Thereupon Captain McKay and the other gentlemen did the same, though the night was very cold.

To the men of New Inverness fortune had been illiberal. Proscribed, landless, and virtually exiled, through participation in the Stuart rising of 1717, they had brought to the Western world little but sturdy strength and steadfast hearts. But the paramount importance of character was proved when, in spite of their disadvantages, they became the outstanding men in Georgia's early history.

The district surrounding New Inverness was called Darien, in memory of the ill-fated Scotch settlement on the Isthmus of Panama, and a little later on this name was given to the town itself. The country was high and healthy, and the lands of inexhaustible fertility. The Mother Country provided tools requisite for the clearing of the forests and the cultivation of the soil. Ample supplies of clothing and blankets were furnished, and monthly rations of food were issued. England was especially generous to Georgia, the youngest of her colonies, and Parliament made annual appropriations for the building and strengthening of her forts, sending over cannon and all the ammunition that was necessary.

All fear of Indian hostility soon vanished from New Inverness. The Scotch and French have at all times had a peculiar faculty for winning the good will and confidence of the savage tribes with whom they have been thrown. The McIntoshes, McKays, and McBains fraternized with the braves of the tribes north and west of the settlement, and soon gained their friendship. The feathered cap, swinging kilt, naked knee, and buskined foot appealed to the innate love of the picturesque that exists in primitive man, and the valor and wild exploits of the Scots excited their admiration. New Inverness became the great rendezvous of the Indians, who frequently brought in game for sale, asking only sixpence for a whole deer, and twopence for a wild turkey weighing forty pounds.

Mr. Thomas Spalding wrote in an article published by the Georgia Historical Society, Volume I, "My grandfather, William McIntosh, oldest son of John Morh, told me that the very best of feeling existed between the young men of New Inverness and the visiting chiefs of the different tribes. They emulated one another in woodcraft and athletic sports, and he said that he himself had never seen the Indian who could beat him with a gun or spear, or pass before him in the hunting field or foot race."

The more adventurous of the young men found employment at the different military posts, as soldiers, guides, or teamsters, and many of them took up hunting as a profession, as the woods swarmed with game and there was a ready sale for the pelts of animals on the trading lines established along the Altamaha.

The lands surrounding New Inverness and the adjacent coast islands were assigned to the colonists, and, as in the Old Country, families settled in the same neighborhood. Black Island was the first grant of land made to John Morh McIntosh, and General's Island to his son Lachlan. To the island grants were annexed landing places on the main, which were often tracts of large extent. The Rice Hope tract on the headwaters of the Sapelo River was granted to John Morh's youngest son, George, and the Court House, near it, to Alexander Baillie, who had married his only daughter, Anna. These two were the first large plantations to be cleared. Between them were Fair Hope and Mallow, which belonged to Lachlan and his brother William, who also owned the Cottage and the Forest tracts. John Morh McIntosh and his four sons, William, Lachlan, John, and George, were known as the Borlam McIntoshes, and their land as the Borlam Land.

The McIntoshes of Bain and the McDonalds settled on the sources of the South Newport River; the McBains, Clarks, and Grants on lands lying to the north of New Inverness.

These Scotch settlers of 1736 were to have almost exclusive possession of the rich river lands in the neighborhood of New Inverness, and of the near-by islands, while the pine lands of the interior were granted in great part to that flotsam of rather undesirable people which is found always to accompany any tide of immigration.

Very early in the life of the colony indigo was planted, and for many years, in the pine lands west of Eulonia, the excavations could still be seen which had been used as vats in which the indigo was steeped and beaten for the extraction of the dye.

Sensible, saving, and hard working, the Scots soon showed the result of their industry in the steady progress made by the colony. The Reverend John McLeod also had labored not vainly or without reward, and by 1742 there was an almost universal adherence to the Presbyterian form of worship in this part of the state. It was not until citizens of South Carolina came later to settle on the Georgia coast that there was any house of worship not presided over by the followers of Calvin and Knox. John McLeod must have been an ideal pastor, as he gave the most careful instruction in religion to his people, and "intermeddled in no other affairs."

By this time the Georgians found themselves at a great disadvantage compared with the Carolinians. Many plantations had been cleared around Savannah and along the coast south of it, and while the Carolinians were reaping large harvests by means of slave labor, the Georgians were unable to cultivate their rich lands, because of the climate so deadly to white labor.

In 1736, an appeal for the employment of slaves was sent to General Oglethorpe by the citizens of Savannah, to save, as they said, the province from ruin. Copies of this appeal were sent to the Germans at Ebenezer and to the Scots at New Inverness, and both refused to sign it.

When we consider the innate love of personal freedom that in all ages has distinguished the mountaineer, a love that seems to have sprung from daily association with nature in its sublimest form, it ought not to surprise us when we find, as early as January 1739, a strong and prophetic petition from the citizens of New Inverness, addressed to the Governor General, praying that he give no ear to the request from Savannah for the repeal of the clause in the Georgia charter forbidding forever the introduction of African slaves.

The fifth clause of the New Inverness petition is as follows: —

It is shocking to human nature that any race of mankind, and *their posterity,* should be sentenced to perpetual slavery. Nor in justice can we think otherwise of it that they are thrown amongst us to be our scourge, *one day or other,* for our sins; and as freedom to them must be as dear as to us, what a scene of horror must it bring about! And the longer it is unexecuted the bloody scene must be the greater.

We therefore for our own sakes, for our wives and posterity, beg your consideration and interest, that, instead of introducing slaves, you will put us in the way to get some of our countrymen, who, with their own labor in time of peace, and our vigilance if we are invaded, with the help of them, will render it a difficult thing to hurt us, or that part of the province we may possess.

This petition was signed by eighteen men of New Inverness, headed by their chief, John Morh McIntosh.

On the roll of honor are the following names : —

JOHN MORH McINTOSH	DAVID CLARK
JOHN McINTOSH	ALEXANDER CLARK
OF LYNVULGIE	
DONALD McDONALD	DONALD CLARK
HUGH MORRISON	JOSEPH BURGESS
JOHN McDONALD	DONALD CLARK, JR.
JOHN McLEAN	ARCHIBALD McBAIN
JOHN McINTOSH	ALEXANDER MUNRO
(SON TO LYNVULGIE)	
JOHN McINTOSH	WILLIAM MUNRO
OF BAIN	
JAMES McKAY	JOHN CUTHBERT

This was the first protest in all history against the employment of slaves, and it was a protest based on humanitarian grounds.

It might be thought that the opposition shown by the Scots of New Inverness to slavery would manifest itself by its rejection, or by a slow adoption, when it was finally established. This would be to underestimate the power of temptation.

The sanction of law, the example of their neighbors, and the natural craving for wealth induced the Highlanders to accept the universal condition of slavery when, in 1749, the system was introduced into Georgia.

Large sums were invested in the purchase of slaves, the river swamps were cleared, diked, and irrigated by the rise of the tide, which also moved the machinery that threshed and pounded the rice.

Rice and cotton were the staple crops, and before many years the country surrounding New Inverness became richly productive, and the primitive Scotch settlement developed into a thriving agricultural community.

III

FREDERICA

WITH New Inverness as a post of reserve, the garrison of which could be transferred to any threatened point, Oglethorpe considered the Colony safe from Indian hostility, and in 1736 began the erection of a fort for protection against the Spaniards.

While the coast below the Altamaha had not been included in the Creek cession, the islands bordering it were indispensable for the safety of the Colony, and Oglethorpe proceeded to annex them. He had formerly made a tour of all the islands, and probably at that time had renamed the island of Ospo Jekyl, after his friend Sir Joseph Jekyl, who had been a generous contributor to the Georgia Colony. At the request of the Indian youth Toonahowie, he called the Island of San Pedro Cumberland. Toonahowie was the adopted son of old Tomocheche, and had been taken to England with his foster parents by Oglethorpe. While there, the Duke of Cumberland, the son of the king, had presented him with a gold watch. The names of the other coast islands were retained, those of St. Catherine's, Sapelo, and St. Simon's becoming Anglicized.

Oglethorpe decided on St. Simon's Island as his best strategic point, for, should the Spaniards attack the Georgia coast, they would come through the broad inland channel between St. Simon's and the mainland, which was navigable for large vessels.

The island was healthy, beautifully wooded, and its soil was rich and fertile. Its forests of oak and pine were interspersed with open savannas or prairies and filled with game, including deer.

Oglethorpe chose for the site of his fort a bluff on the western side of the island, where there had been an old Indian field about forty acres in extent. The bluff stood ten feet above high water, and the soil was dry and sandy. The fort, located on a bend which was known as the Devil's Elbow, would command the river, which entered the ocean lower down through Jekyl Sound.

In addition to the fort, Oglethorpe decided to build a town, which was to be the seat of government of the Georgia Colony, and this he called Frederica after Frederick, Prince of Wales, the son of George II.

In February the soldiers were set to work clearing the site for the new town, the circumference of which was to be about one and a half miles. Surrounding it was a wall ten feet high, faced with timber, outside of which was a deep ditch, with gates to admit tide water. On the river was a water battery. On the land side were two bastions, the foundation of one being still in existence. The two entrance gates were called the Town and Water Posts, the former being surmounted by a bell which apprised the garrison whenever the gate was opened.

The town was laid off with streets which crossed at right angles, and these were planted with rows of orange trees and named after the officers. High Street, which led off into the country, was twenty-five yards wide. There were no squares in the little town, but there was an esplanade, and outside, on the east, was a parade ground.

Each man was given a lot sixty by ninety feet, on which temporary booths were erected, fourteen by twenty feet. These were neatly thatched with palmetto leaves, and, standing in regular rows, looked like a camp. Three large tents belonging to Oglethorpe and Captain Horton were pitched on the Parade near the river.

By May, the soldiers began making brick and sawing wood for building. The fort and garrison buildings were made of tabby. Two of these were to be used for barracks, and next to the Water Post was the guardhouse, under which was the prison. Twenty-seven brick houses, some of them quite handsome, were erected for the officers.

South of Frederica was a wood, which was used for fuel and pasturage and which served as a screen, hiding the fort from vessels coming up the river. In front of the wood was a battery of twelve guns, protected by a miry marsh. Four miles farther down was Gascoigne's Bluff, where Captain James Gascoigne had his headquarters, as head of the navy.

On the south point of the island, Oglethorpe erected Fort St. Simon's. Here a battery was planted and barracks built for troops, with a watch-tower to discover vessels at sea. Should one be sighted, an alarm gun was to be fired, the number of shots indicating the number of ships, while a horseman was to ride posthaste to Frederica, about nine miles distant, with the news. The lighthouse now stands near this spot, and the old ruins still discernible are supposed to be those of the chapel of an old Spanish mission.

On the north end of St. Simon's Island a corporal's guard was kept at Pike's Bluff, and on the east Lieutenant Delegal commanded the King's Independent Company at Fort Delegal.

From Frederica, Oglethorpe built a military road leading down to Fort St. Simon's. Running southeast from the town, the road entered a beautiful prairie, a mile in extent. Then, crossing the island through the woods, still in the same direction, it came out on the eastern marshes, which it skirted to within two miles of the fort. Here there was a bend in crescent form, and the road followed a southwesterly direction to the point.

Oglethorpe did not live at Frederica, but had his establishment east of it, where the road entered the prairie. His simple frame cottage, with its surrounding edifices, looked like a neat little country village. On the fifty acres reserved was a large garden, and an orchard of figs and grapes. The house, overshadowed by oaks, looked westward across the prairie upon the town and fort, where the beautiful white houses of Frederica seemed raised "as by an enchanter's will." This modest establishment, which he called Orange Hall, was the only home ever owned by General Oglethorpe in the new world.

In addition to fortifying St. Simon's, Oglethorpe erected barracks at the north end of Jekyl Island, where he stationed a garrison. On the

RUINS OF FORT FREDERICA, ST. SIMON'S ISLAND

RUINS OF THE SLAVE QUARTERS, SAPELO ISLAND

north end of Cumberland a small post, Fort Andrews, was built to protect inland navigation, and
on the south end Fort William, a work of considerable strength, commanded the entrance to St.
Mary's. Fort George was built at the mouth of
the St. John's, as Oglethorpe was determined to
keep the Spaniards south of that river. All of
these fortifications were built within eleven months.

On his first return from England, Oglethorpe
had brought back with him two young clergymen
of the Church of England, John and Charles Wesley. John Wesley took charge of Christ Church
in Savannah, while Charles, as secretary to Oglethorpe, came down to Frederica. In his journal
he writes: "Tuesday, March 9th, 1736, about 3 in
the afternoon, I first set foot on St. Simon's Island,
and immediately my spirit revived. The people
seemed overjoyed to see me. Mr. Oglethorpe in
particular received me very kindly."

The people of Frederica were at this time living
in the palmetto-thatched booths, and services had
to be held on the Parade, "a carpet of grass beneath
the great live-oaks." Charles Wesley conducted
four religious services a day, the drum summoning
the people to worship, and he writes in his journal,
"I preached with boldness."

It was on that same carpet of grass that the ladies

of the town gave Mr. Wesley great offense, "by a too often, and too great flaunting of their gowns." And gowns could be "flaunted" in those days, consisting, as they did, of voluminous skirts, tight bodices, and flowing sleeves, of lutestring or taffeta. What so shocked the saintly young man must have been a pretty sight, as the gay ladies strolled on the green grass beneath the great oaks and drifting gray moss.

Charles Wesley only stayed on the island seventy days, and most of this time was spent in wrangling. "On the 16th General Oglethorpe set out with the Indians for the main to hunt the buffalo," he writes. At this time there were said to be ten thousand buffalo between Darien and Sapelo River. "On the evening of the 18th," Wesley continues, "M. W. discovered to me the whole mystery of iniquity." Who the busybody M. W. was is not known. In his *Life of Oglethorpe,* Bruce says, "As usual there was a woman, or rather two women in it. Both claiming to have Oglethorpe as their protector and patron. They carry themselves in the little society with great freedom."

On Oglethorpe's return, Wesley undertook to censure him, which so angered the General that he used language hardly consistent with his usually gracious manner. The young man was cut and scorned on all sides, and in his diary he wrote, "Woe is me that I am still constrained to dwell with Meshech!" Oglethorpe, however, relented, softened toward one who had only his prayers for his comfort, and they parted as friends when the General and Captain McIntosh left to reconnoitre the Spanish lands. On Oglethorpe's return they met with all differences forgotten, Charles Wesley saying, "I longed, sir, upon your leaving, to see you once more, that I might tell you some things, but I considered should you die you would know them all." To which Oglethorpe, broad-minded and big-hearted, replied, "I know not whether separated spirits regard our little concerns. If they do, it is as men regard the follies of their childhood."

John Wesley visited Frederica once while his brother was there, but Charles's stay was short, for on May 15 he set out for Savannah, and Oglethorpe could have hardly regretted his departure. A great oak not far from the site of Frederica, under which Wesley is said to have preached, is still pointed out.

Charles Wesley stayed only a short time in Savannah, leaving for England on July 26, having preached on the previous Sunday from the text, "Let us arise and go hence." After his departure John visited St. Simon's twice, and then gave it up.

"Having beaten the air in this unhappy place," he writes, "for 20 days, I took my final leave of Frederica. It was not any apprehension of my own danger, but an utter despair of doing good there, which made me content with seeing it no more." The following year John Wesley left Savannah. Although the Methodist Church was founded later on by these two devout and gifted, but tactless, young men, they never left the Church of England.

The Spaniards in Florida were naturally incensed by the building of so many fortifications on land which they considered their own, and in the fall of 1736 they demanded, at Frederica and in London, the immediate evacuation of all territory south of St. Helena Sound. Realizing the gravity of the situation, Oglethorpe sailed for England to dispute the Spanish claims, and to secure assistance for the Colony. In less than a year he returned to Frederica as Commander in Chief of His Majesty's forces, bringing with him upwards of seven hundred well-equipped men. To attach these soldiers to the colony they were to defend, permission had been given to each man to bring his wife, and additional pay and rations were provided for this purpose.

Oglethorpe landed with these troops at Soldiers'

Fort, on the south end of St. Simon's Island, on September 19, 1737, where they were saluted by all the cannon. Coming up to Frederica, they were again saluted by fifteen guns from the fort and welcomed by all the townsmen, headed by the magistrates, Frederica having the same municipal government as Savannah.

In the event of war with Spain, Oglethorpe realized the importance of securing the friendship of the Creek Indians, and he now made a perilous journey to Coweta on the Chattahoochee, four hundred miles north of Frederica, where a great Indian council was being held. Besides his servants, he took with him only three men, and a halfblood woman, named Mary Musgrove, to act as his interpreter. This was giving the highest proof of courage, as he was exposed to the treachery of any Indian who might covet the rich reward which would have been given by the Spaniards for his capture. The Creeks thought so highly of Oglethorpe's courage that they received him cordially, and he smoked their pipe of peace, drank their war medicine, and was initiated into their mysteries.

In the conference that followed, the Creeks declared that they had always owned the land from the Savannah to the St. Mary's River, and would allow no one but the English to settle on it. A treaty was made granting them the land along the coast between the Altamaha and the St. Mary's "as high as the tide flowed."

In December 1739, England declared war against Spain, and Oglethorpe made preparations to invade Florida. He had information that St. Augustine was poorly manned and in need of supplies, and he decided to attack it before it could be reënforced. The Highland Rangers of New Inverness, commanded by their captain, John Morh McIntosh, came at the first call, and these were joined by a regiment of four hundred men from Virginia and South Carolina. Oglethorpe with one body of troops went down by boat through the inland channels, expecting the land force to join him on the Florida coast by a certain date.

William McIntosh, the oldest son of John Morh, who was at this time not quite fourteen, wished to accompany his father, but was refused permission. He pursued the column and overtook it at Barrington, and his father sent him back next day with an armed guard. The boy then took a small boat and rowed up the Altamaha to a bluff, where he fell in with some Indians who had known him at New Inverness. He had learned something of their language, and he told them of his plan to trail the Rangers until they reached the St. Mary's

River. The Indians took up his cause with enthusiasm, and together they followed the troops, the
Indians scouting ahead and reporting to young Mc-
Intosh everything that passed in the white man's
camp, while carefully concealing his presence
among them. At last the St. Mary's was crossed,
when, with much triumph, the Indians led him to
his father, saying that he was a young warrior who
would fight, and that the Great Spirit would watch
over his life, for he loved young warriors. The
father relented, and the boy was given the coveted
comradeship.

Owing to the difficulty of their route, the land
force failed to meet Oglethorpe at the appointed
time, which was fatal for the expedition. As soon
as they joined forces, however, they marched on
St. Augustine, and reaching Fort Moosa, two miles
from the town, attacked and took it. Leaving
Captain McIntosh in charge, Oglethorpe went on
to St. Augustine. Unfortunately, by this time
Spanish ships had reached the fort and supplied
it with men and provisions, and he was unable to
capture it.

Meanwhile the Spaniards had surprised the garrison left at Fort Moosa, as it slept, and massacred
thirty-six men. William McIntosh never left his
father's side until he saw him fall, covered with

many wounds. Transfixed with horror, he was not aroused until a Spanish officer laid hold of his plaid. Light and elastic as a steel bow, the boy slipped from the Spaniard's grasp and, making his escape with the wreck of the corps, was one of the twenty-six survivors who returned to the Altamaha.

Captain McIntosh was not killed, but was taken prisoner and sent later on to Spain, where he remained in captivity until released in 1744.

The failure of the expedition against St. Augustine was a blow to the colonists of South Carolina and Georgia, and Oglethorpe was bitterly criticized. But when he attacked St. Augustine he was not fighting an insignificant power. Spain was at this time the greatest of all European countries, and Florida was supported by the whole strength of the Catholic kingdom.

Determined to retake the land that had belonged to them, the Spaniards now began to concentrate their forces at Havana, and by 1742 were ready to attack the Georgia coast.

Oglethorpe awaited the coming contest with some anxiety. He realized that the lower islands and the region of the Altamaha would have to bear the first shock of conflict. Frederica was garrisoned by a part of his own regiment. A company was stationed at Fort St. Simon's, and one each on Jekyl and Cumberland Islands.

To facilitate escape from St. Simon's, should it be necessary, a canal was dug through General's Island just above, making a short cut to New Inverness. There is a tradition that General Oglethorpe, finding himself hemmed in by the Spaniards at New Inverness, ordered his officers to cut a canal through General's Island. This they did with their swords, in a single night! And through this canal Oglethorpe and his men are said to have escaped to St. Simon's, five miles below. The canal, straight as an arrow across the little island, is known as General's Cut. and is used to this day.

For two years an armada, huge for that time, had been assembling in Cuba. It consisted of fifty ships, and carried a force of over five thousand men, commanded by Don Manuel de Monteano. Hearing of its approach, the planters who had established themselves along the Georgia coast abandoned their plantations, and fled with their families to Charleston.

Oglethorpe had made what preparations he could. He had sent a ship to the West Indies to inform Admiral Vernon of the expected invasion, and he had requested aid from South Carolina. Both appeals were ignored, and he was left to his own resources. The remnant of the Highland Rangers, and the Skidaway Scouts from Savannah, thirty men under Captain Noble Jones, came to his assistance, and as soon as his Indian allies received word of the impending conflict, they hastened to the coast and crossed to Frederica.

By the time that three brigs could be armed, the Spanish armada was at the mouth of the St. Mary's, and on the twenty-first of June, 1742, nine Spanish vessels came into Amelia Sound and demanded the surrender of Fort William. Ensign Stuart, who commanded it, replied that he would neither surrender nor be taken. The Spaniards attempted to land, but were repulsed, and, Oglethorpe coming to Stuart's relief, the enemy put to sea with considerable loss. Reënforcing Fort William, Oglethorpe returned to Frederica, where, with a force of only 652 soldiers, he awaited the arrival of his formidable foe.

On the twenty-eighth of June, thirty-six Spanish vessels anchored off St. Simon's bar, where they remained until the fifth of July, sending in small vessels to sound the channel. On this day they came in at flood tide, under a brisk fire from the battery of Fort St. Simon's, and, passing it, sailed up to Gascoigne's Bluff. Fort St. Simon's was then abandoned, and the garrison, after spiking the guns, marched to Frederica.

Landing at Gascoigne's Bluff, the Spaniards erected a battery, and the next day attempted to attack Frederica by water, but were repulsed by the battery of guns in the woods in front of it.

Oglethorpe kept scouting parties out, watching every move of the enemy, while his main body worked hard on the fortifications of Frederica. Day and night the Indians scoured the woods and brought in many prisoners, who informed Oglethorpe of the number of their forces. The report was ominous, but, still hoping for reënforcements from South Carolina, the General did all that he could to keep up the spirits of his troops.

The Spaniards made several attempts to attack Frederica by land, but were repulsed, and in one encounter a number of Spaniards were killed and taken prisoners, among them being Captain Sanchez, who was afterwards exchanged for Captain John Morh McIntosh.

Not long after this a Frenchman deserted from Frederica, and fearing that he would reveal the weakness of the fort to the enemy, Oglethorpe resorted to strategy. He wrote a letter to the traitor telling him to inform the Spaniards of their position, and to urge them to attack Frederica, adding that he was about to receive reënforcements from Charleston of six British ships of war. This letter was given to a Spanish prisoner, who was set at liberty on condition that he would give it privately to the Frenchman. The prisoner gave it, as he was expected to do, to the Spanish commander. A council of war was immediately called, and Monteano decided to attack Frederica before reënforcements could arrive.

Captain Noble Jones, who was out with a scouting party, fell in with some of the enemy's patrols, and captured them. From these prisoners it was learned that the whole Spanish army was advancing along the road from Fort St. Simon's to Frederica. Oglethorpe at once dispatched forces to meet it, the main command being under Captain Raymond Demaré.

Reaching the turn or crescent of the road near the marsh, which has been known ever since as Bloody Marsh, the Spaniards broke rank, stacked arms, and, taking out their kettles, prepared to cook dinner.

About this time Captain Sutherland's Company of Regulars, and the Highland Rangers under Captain McKay, reached the turn of the road, and concealed themselves in the dense, vine-entangled woods. From this position they could see the Spaniards, and, realizing that they were off guard, they decided on an immediate attack. Captain McKay occupied the rather high ground where the Postell house afterward stood; Captain Sutherland the woods, where the monument has since been erected.

Upon a signal a heavy fire was opened on the Spaniards, who were thrown into the utmost confusion. They sprang to arms, but were shot down by the British, who were invisible to them; and, after repeated efforts to re-form, they fled. Numbers were killed, and many were hunted down by the Indians, who, on hearing the firing, had come on a run through the woods, to be in at the death. The marsh was covered with the dead and dying, and few Spaniards regained their camp. The loss in killed, wounded, and prisoners was estimated at five hundred.

Tradition says that Oglethorpe knew by the sound of the muskets that they were fired by his own victorious troops, and that, hastening to the field, he ordered a wagonload of porter to refresh his soldiers. The bottles were broken in a heap on the battlefield, as a monument, but have since been buried in the sand.

Don Manuel de Monteano did not abandon the invasion of St. Simon's because of this defeat, but because he feared the arrival of a strong fleet of war vessels from Carolina, which might cut off his retreat to Florida or Cuba. He burned all of the works on the south end of the island, and also the residence of Major Horton on Jekyl; and then, sailing south, he camped on the north end of Cumberland, at Fort St. Andrews. The next day Oglethorpe pursued the Spaniards, who put to sea, and the Georgia Colony was saved on the brink of destruction.

Because of its far-reaching importance, the battle of Bloody Marsh ranks as one of the decisive battles of the world, and St. Simon's has been called the Thermopylæ of the Southern Provinces. "The deliverance of Georgia from the Spaniards," said Whitfield, the famous preacher, "is such as can not be paralleled but by some instance out of the Old Testament."

Though the Spaniards had been fifteen days on St. Simon's, during which time there had been constant skirmishing, the losses of the British were comparatively light. When the war was over, an exchange of prisoners took place and Captain Sanchez was exchanged for John Morh McIntosh. Communication between the two countries was so slow, however, that it was not until 1744 that General McIntosh, aged and broken by his confinement, returned to his Georgia home.

The rest of his life was spent at the Grove, his place near Darien, and most of his time was passed resting in the shade of a great oak, on the bank of a creek. This tree was always known as John Morh McIntosh's Oak, and was still alive in 1882, when it was more than seven feet in diameter.

In 1743, Oglethorpe decided to give up his command and return to England. He had spent ten years in the service of the Colony, crossing the Atlantic six times. During his stay he had given large sums from his private funds, and added not one dollar to his fortune. Excepting the modest home on St. Simon's, not an acre was reserved for himself of the thousands of square miles that, through him, were sold or ceded to the white man by the Indian.

James Edward Oglethorpe was the embodiment of courage and resolution, and had the rare power of inspiring with his own spirit all who acted under him. Indian hostility was transformed by his presence into friendly association, and hostile savage tribes became faithful and devoted allies. Distances were not measured, or hardships considered, if his presence was to be of advantage to those he had led into this new world. His labors were great, and his life was noble. Returning to England, he lived to an honored old age, dying in 1785 at the age of eighty-nine.

On Oglethorpe's departure from St. Simon's his regiment was disbanded. Many of the soldiers remained in the Colony, and were the ancestors of men who afterwards became prominent in the social life of the Georgia coast.

IV

THROUGH THE REVOLUTION

On Oglethorpe's departure, Major Horton took command of all the troops in the Georgia Colony, and during his administration won the esteem and friendship of the best people in the province. Major Horton had been the first Englishman to settle on Jekyl Island, where he cleared a large acreage on which he raised hops and grain for the brewery at the north end, which supplied the soldiers with excellent beer. (The English officers drank more ardent spirits, unless in the presence of their General.) He also planted ten thousand orange trees in rows along the island, and built a comfortable tabby house. The ruins of his home, which was destroyed during the Spanish occupation, are still in existence.

After the defeat of the Spaniards, the military posts on Cumberland Island were abandoned as unnecessary, and later on it became the home of wealthy planters. Jekyl alone remained a military reservation until 1766, when it was granted by the crown to Clement Martin.

The years that followed were the palmy days of Frederica, as the garrison was stationed there. The little town was noted for its neatness and the beauty of its parades, and at this time was a very gay place.

The trade in furs and peltries with the Indian tribes to the north and south had been established, ships cleared from England directly to Frederica, and prosperity followed. On the island were about two hundred homes and a thousand inhabitants, exclusive of the soldiers.

The first land grants were given to discharged soldiers, artisans, and storekeepers, men of moderate means, and cotton planting began on a small scale, the wives of the soldiers spinning and knitting stockings from the cotton.

The island was healthy, the woods and sea gave food in profusion, and the town furnished a ready market for all that could be raised on the little farms. These were worked by the older men, while the younger ones found employment as boatmen or laborers for the military administration, some as clerks or purveyors to the camps, blockhouses, or other military stations.

"On St. Simon's," writes an early historian,

"civilization and the arts were introduced, while all around was nature in her wildest mood."

In the woods these first settlers found delicious wild grapes which had probably survived from the vineyards of the Franciscan Fathers. Orange trees also remained, and the story is told of the Scotchman who saw one for the first time covered with its golden fruit. He attempted to climb the tree, but finding it impossible because of its sharp thorns, he cut it down to secure the oranges.

One of the first large grants on St. Simon's was that of a thousand acres on the eastern side of the island. This was given to a set of Moravians, who had offered their services to Oglethorpe in defense of the colony. Captain Hermsdorf, their leader, had been one of Oglethorpe's most trusted officers, and all of the men had won the respect of the community. In taking up arms they had broken a religious law of their sect, and fearing that their brethren in Ebenezer would give them no cordial reception, they decided after the war to stay on St. Simon's.

On the tract allotted them they built a hamlet which they called the Village, and began cultivating the land and planting mulberry trees for the rearing of silkworms. They were a quiet, industrious people, and their neat little town was made attractive by the planting of vines, figs, and oranges around their homes. A Lutheran church was built, their first pastor being the Reverend John Ulrick Dreisler. He died and was buried at Frederica, being succeeded by the Reverend Mr. Zubli from Switzerland. Probably to join more of their kind, the Moravians left St. Simon's in 1748 and moved to Pennsylvania, when the Village was bought by George Baillie.

St. Simon's was peopled almost entirely by men of Scotch nativity, and its lands in large measure were granted to the McKays, Cuthberts, Grants, and McIntoshes, all connected by blood or marriage with the colonists of New Inverness. When the leaders of that outpost declared to the world "the Creed" under which they hoped to live, their kinsmen of St. Simon's remained silent. The military importance of Frederica and their growing prosperity had developed a love of trade and a desire for an easy life. Material rewards quickly appeared, the population of the island increased, and wealth, as then measured, came as a result of direct trade with the Mother Country.

However, much of the island was still covered with virgin wood, and no great number of slaves had yet been introduced to further the clearance of the land.

Among the larger grants on St. Simon's was that
of Captain James McKay, whose tract of eight
hundred acres on the northeast end was afterwards
known as Cannon's Point. He also owned the
lands of St. Clair just below it, where he built his
home. At St. Clair grew the great oak which
was known as "Old England."   No tree in Georgia or Carolina could for a moment compare with
it, for girth, grandeur, and spread of limb. Defi-
ant of time, wind, and storms, it stood strong
and green until 1857, succumbing only to fire. To-
day its dead limbs stretch sixty feet on every side of
a trunk about eight feet in diameter.

James McKay was an eccentric character. He
declined the title of Baron Reay, which he inherited
in Scotland, passing his claim on, in some mysterious way, to his younger brother Hugh, who returned to the Old Country.

He was a man of mild and gentlemanly manners,
but of a decided, not to say stubborn, character.
He had a royal commission, being Captain in His
Majesty's 42nd Regiment, the Black Watch. Ordered with his company to western Virginia to co-
operate with one Colonel Washington in an attack
on Fort Duquesne, he forgot to marry Miss Ann
McIntosh of Bain. Possibly Miss McIntosh ex-
plains the refusal of the family title. When he

reached Virginia, Captain McKay refused to take orders from a provincial colonel, and his company occupied a separate encampment. There was no personal difficulty, however. Washington and he became good friends, and he died in 1792 at Washington's home in Alexandria.

Miss Ann McIntosh was left a life interest in St. Clair and in all the property that Captain McKay owned in Georgia, with remainder in fee simple to her only daughter, Ann McKay McIntosh. For some unknown reason the lady was always known as Mrs. Rainbow McIntosh.

A grant of a thousand acres at the northwest end of the island was given to Mr. Ladsden of Charleston, who called the place Hampton.

One of the most attractive homes on St. Simon's at this time was that of Captain Raymond Demaré, who was one of Oglethorpe's oldest officers. He was a wealthy Huguenot, and, deciding to live on the island, he built his house a half mile due east of Orange Hall, and called it Harrington Hall. Much of his fortune was spent on ornamenting his place in the French style. The house was said to be "conspicuous for its beauty and comfort," and the grounds were inclosed by hedges of *Ilex cassine* or Christmas berry. This beautiful shrub, which grows to a height of twenty feet, has small glossy leaves of a bright green, and in the autumn bears vermilion berries of waxen softness that are almost transparent.   The Coast Indians dried the leaves of this shrub to sell to the Indians of upper Georgia, who made from them a ceremonial drink for their chiefs, war captains and priests.

The two oldest sons of John Morh McIntosh, William and Lachlan, had been taken into Oglethorpe's regiment as cadets when quite young, and served with the Highlanders at the battle of Bloody Marsh; William being just sixteen.   Later on, when he became a distinguished soldier in the Revolution, the tract of land surrounding this spot was granted to him.

At this time there was living in Frederica one Thomas Bosomworth, who had come from England as Chaplain in Oglethorpe's Regiment.   He had married the half-breed, Mary Musgrove, Oglethorpe's faithful friend and interpreter, and under his baleful influence her character had completely changed.   Bosomworth was avaricious and unscrupulous, and he had married Mary hoping to obtain vast possessions.

In December 1747, Melatche, a Creek chieftain whom Mary claimed as her half brother, visited Frederica with sixteen other micos or kings.   Bosomworth managed to have Melatche crowned Emperor of the Creeks, and then induced him to bestow on his sister the Hunting Islands, Ossabaw, St. Catherine's, and Sapelo. A deed to these islands was signed "on the fourth day of the Windy Moon," giving them to Mary "as long as the sun shall shine, and the waters run in the rivers."

As soon as the Colonial authorities heard of this transaction they notified the Bosomworths that the cession of so great a part of the province would not be allowed. Fortified by drink, and accompanied by a warlike set of Indians, the two marched to Savannah to demand their rights. They were captured and imprisoned, and forced thereafter to resort to law instead of violence to prove their claim. After years of controversy, the London Council ordered the sale of Ossabaw and Sapelo to the highest bidders, and confirmed the title of St. Catherine's to the Bosomworths. Moving to that island, they built a substantial house of hickory logs, plastered inside and out and surrounded by a spacious piazza, and here the precious couple spent the rest of their lives, being buried on the island when they died.

When in 1749 slavery was introduced into the Georgia Colony, many planters from Virginia and the Carolinas bought and developed large plantations along the coast. Audley Maxwell, who was

known as Maxwell of Medway, came from Penn-
sylvania, and settled with his family at the head of
Medway River. He was followed by his brother
James, and the two were valuable acquisitions to
Georgia, holding many important positions in the
Colony.

In 1752, a band of New England Puritans who
had originally settled in Dorchester, South Carolina, moved to the Georgia coast, and established Medway, halfway between Darien and
Savannah.

As both of these places were at a considerable
distance, the people of this neighborhood now decided to build a town for themselves, and Sunbury
was laid out in a beautiful situation on St. Catherine's Sound. With a fine harbor, the little town
grew so rapidly that by 1770 it rivaled Savannah
in importance.

From this time on until the Revolution there was
increasing prosperity all along the Georgia coast.
Generous gifts of land were made to all incoming
settlers, and the fresh lands yielded abundantly.
Planters who had worn out their lands in more
northern states came down with their slaves and
families, and Georgia increased more rapidly in
population than any of her sister colonies.

"I doubt if anywhere within the circle of British

civilization," Charles Wylly writes in his *Memories,* "such picturesque contrasts of social conditions could have been found, as in the narrow circle of early Georgia. In Savannah might be met the loose-living English adventurer, the men of Fielding's novels. A few miles to the west, the steady German tilled his fields at Ebenezer, under his pastor and teacher. But a day's ride to the South, a band of Puritans of strictest tenets had planted their stakes at Medway Church; whilst farther south, on the very frontier of the colony, their moral antipodes would be found in the fervid Celt. And among them all, at that time free and friendly, roamed the Red Man of the woods.

"By the Treaty of Paris in 1763, Florida was ceded by Spain to Great Britain. To Darien and Frederica this brought a crucial change. Up to this time they had been the vital points in the defense of the Southern Colonies. They had been garrisoned by regular forces or by volunteers, mustered into the service of the King. Now they found themselves relegated to insignificance and blotted off the military chart, for forts were no longer needed for defense against the Spaniards. Darien and Frederica had shared the advantages that come from military occupation and expenditure, and now they were thrown on their own re-

THROUGH THE REVOLUTION 63

sources. The result was very different in the two places.

"In Darien the Highland Rangers were disbanded. The drum and pipes no longer sounded on the banks of the Altamaha, where from now until 1776 the English flag was to wave only on festal days of peace, and not as heretofore over men marshaled for battlefield and fray. But in spite of what it lost as a military post, Darien prospered, and grew with the steady progress that thrift and industry ensure. The surrounding lands were rich, the grazing unlimited, and the people safe from Spanish or Indian hostilities. Additions to the number of settlers were constant, some coming from the parent country and others from Carolina and the Northern provinces.

"In these years the Georgia coast may be said to have attained its legal majority, taking its place as a responsible unit in the government of the Colony of Georgia. Before, it had been an outpost of the Governor General's, owing allegiance to the representatives of the Crown, and not until 1751 had it been granted representation in the annual assemblies of the Colonial Council."

While Darien prospered, Frederica declined. Soon after 1763 the fort was dismantled, and the garrison withdrawn to St. Augustine. Gone forever was the gay life, the neat trimness of a military town, and its ephemeral prosperity. "It presents the melancholy prospect of houses without inhabitants, barracks without soldiers, guns without carriages, and streets growing over with weeds," writes a journalist. "All appeared to me with a horrible aspect, so different from what I once knew it, that I could scarce refrain from tears."

Between 1760 and 1775 every foot of Frederica was acquired by purchase by Donald McKay.

Donald McKay had married Jean Gordon, both of the original Scotch immigration, and their only daughter, Katherine, became the wife of her cousin, William McIntosh. Their home was on the Borlam lands near Darien, a home in which were found "all the virtues, besides the influence of religion." The McIntoshes had several sons and an only daughter, Margery, who was the great favorite of her grandfather, Donald McKay of Frederica.

In 1760, James Spalding, a young Scotchman twenty-five years of age, arrived on St. Simon's Island. Born in County Perth, he was heir to the estate and barony of Ashantilly. Having some means, he entered into partnership with Donald McKay. The trading post which they established was a branch of the great house of Blanton Forbes and Company, which brought cargoes directly from

England and sold them to the Indian tribes that lived as far north as the Tennessee and as far south as the Everglades of Florida, the goods being carried by pony train. Their storehouses extended from Sunbury, Georgia, to Valusia, Florida, and their canoes floated to and from Frederica, the central storehouse.

Lachlan McIntosh was at this time chief magistrate of Frederica, and it is probable that the charming Margery McIntosh often visited her grandfather and Uncle Lachlan when she became a young lady, and in this way met the successful young business man, James Spalding. They fell in love, and in 1772 were married, her grandfather giving Frederica to Margery as a marriage portion. The first home of the young couple was at Orange Hall, James Spalding having bought Oglethorpe's "little property," and here, in 1774, their only son, Thomas, was born.

It was in this year that William Bartram, the famous naturalist, visited the South for the second time. Landing at Sunbury, he had attended services at the Medway Church, then gone on down to Broughton Island, where he was hospitably entertained by its owner, General Laurens of South Carolina. On the banks of the Altamaha he collected many native plants, and discovered the *Gordonia lascianthus,* which has since been known as the *Gordonia altamaha.* This beautiful flowering plant grows only on a few acres on the banks of this river, and Bartram found it nowhere else on his travels as far as the Mississippi. He transplanted it to his famous garden in Philadelphia, and sent it also to the Botanical Gardens in London.

Bartram stopped at many homes along the coast, and was always hospitably received. "Crossing the Sapelo," he writes, "and a mile distant, I stopped at Mr. Alexander Baillie's (now Eulonia), to deliver a letter from the Governor. He invited me to stay with him, but I continued on to the home of Mr. William McIntosh, about a mile farther. The beautiful woods presented a view of magnificence inexpressibly charming and animating. When I came to Mr. McIntosh's door, the friendly man, smiling, and with a grace and dignity peculiar to himself, took me by the hand, and accosted me thus: 'Friend Bartram, come under my roof, and I desire you to make my home your home as long as convenient to yourself. Remember that from this moment you are a part of my family, and on my part, I shall endeavor to make it agreeable.' I shall mention a remarkable instance of Mr. McIntosh's friendship and respect for me, which was recommending his eldest son, Mr. John McIntosh, as companion in my travels.   He was a sensible, virtuous youth, and a very agreeable companion through a long and tiresome journey of near a thousand miles."

Bartram was naturally "forwarded" to his daughter's home on St. Simon's by Mr. McIntosh, and of this visit he writes: —

I arrived at Frederica on the island of St. Simon's, where I was well received and entertained by Mr. James Spalding.   A very large part of the island had formerly been cleared and planted by the English, as appeared by vestiges of plantations, ruins of costly buildings, highways, etc.   Frederica was the first fort built by the English in Georgia.   It was regular and beautiful, and was perhaps the largest and most costly of any in North America, of British construction.   The ruins of the town only remain; peach trees, figs, pomegranates, and other shrubs grow out of the ruinous walls of former spacious and expensive buildings. There are a few neat houses in good repair and inhabited.   The island seems to be recovering again, owing to the liberal spirit of J. Spalding, Esqr., who is President of the island, and engaged in extensive mercantile concerns.

From Mr. Spalding Bartram obtained the letters which secured for him the courtesies of many gentlemen in Florida and Alabama.

But for the Revolution it is possible that James Spalding might have succeeded in reviving St. Simon's, although at this time there were only fifteen families residing on the island.

By the seventies unrest was spreading all over America, as the Colonies realized how unfairly they were treated by the Mother Country. Georgia alone had no cause for complaint, as England had been most generous to her youngest colony. But even in Georgia there was discontent. Political opinions differed, and families became divided in principle.

The year 1775 found the coast torn by discord, and when the Revolution came, many Georgians remained loyal to Great Britain.

James Spalding was one of these. He and George McIntosh, the youngest son of John Morh, endeavored to remain neutral, always a dangerous course at such a time. Finding, however, that it was not possible to stem the tide, Mr. Spalding removed with his wife and son to Florida, where he stayed until the Revolution was over, devoting himself during this time to the personal education of his son.

The coast of Georgia was exposed to military inroads from the new British possession of Florida, and was ravaged from end to end, the enemy plundering, burning, and murdering in every home not defended by strong arms.

George McIntosh resided at Rice Hope on the Borlam lands. In spite of his loyalty to the crown, his home was burned, his Negroes run off and sold, his barns and property destroyed. A letter from him, written on July 3, 1777, reads like words from an old border story: —

"They have taken possession of my estate, destroyed my crops, by turning their horses on to them, killed and driven off my stock, of every kind, broke open my house, barn and cellar, plundered and carried off everything of value they could find, wantonly committing every act of waste and destruction." Two days later he writes, "I am just informed one of my most trusty Negroes, on my indigo place, has been cruelly whipped, until he died in the rope, because he would not tell my hiding place." And he adds, "Excuse this handwriting, for it is done on my knee, and under a tree in my own woods."

It was Governor Gwinnet's approval of the treatment of George McIntosh which led to the duel with Colonel Lachlan McIntosh, his brother. Both duelists were thought to be fatally wounded, and Gwinnet died an hour later. Lachlan McIntosh recovered and was transferred to the North, where he served under Washington at Valley Forge. He became a Brigadier General in the Continental army, won the personal esteem of his great chief, and lived to receive President Washington as his guest when he visited Savannah in 1791.

The two other McIntosh brothers, William and John, distinguished themselves during the Revolution. Indeed, for his gallant defense of Fort Morris — which protected Sunbury — the Georgia legislature voted that a sword should be presented to Colonel John McIntosh, on which were engraved the words, "Come and Take It!" — his answer to the British who demanded its surrender.

During the Revolution Frederica was taken by the British vessels that lay in the sound. Its fort was dismantled, the barracks burned, its inhabitants dispersed, and gradually what had been the gay and thriving garrison town crumbled into ruins.

When James Spalding returned from Florida after the Revolution, he found his storehouses rifled and burned, and everything of value that he possessed scattered to the winds. All the accumulations of a lifetime of thrift and industry were destroyed, and he was all but a ruined man.

Many others were in the same condition, but

with courage and determination they went to work to repair their broken fortunes. What little capital still existed, or could be borrowed, was invested in planting sea-island cotton, which had been introduced from the Island of Anguilla in the West Indies. It was planted first on St. Simon's Island, and its cultivation spread rapidly to the mainland.

Immigrants from North and South Carolina began coming again to the Georgia coast, and French refugees from the West Indies added their courtesy and culture to the energy of the Scotch and English, who up to this time had constituted the whole population. New lands were cleared and dyked, schools and churches were built, and by the close of the century the ruins that marked the end of the war were hidden by the growths of peace.

Only the two little towns of Frederica and Sunbury failed to share in the general advance. After the Revolution the trade of Sunbury went to Savannah, and it declined in importance. Gradually it was abandoned by its inhabitants, its deserted houses fell into ruin and disappeared, and nothing now remains but the site.

Truly are these two called "the dead cities of Georgia."

V

ST. SIMON'S ISLAND

In 1795, the life on St. Simon's changed from its primitive state, as the land passed from the possession of small farmers into the hands of a very different class.

In 1793, Mr. John Couper bought the northeast end of the island, which had belonged to Captain James McKay, and settled at Cannon's Point. His friend and partner, Mr. James Hamilton, purchased a number of small tracts at Gascoigne's Bluff, combining them into a plantation which he called Hamilton, on which he placed one hundred slaves. In 1795, Major Pierce Butler bought, from Mr. Ladsden of Charleston, the Hampton Point tract on the northwest point of the island, and from James Mackintosh an adjoining tract of the same acreage. As Mr. James Spalding of Orange Grove died about this time, his eight-hundred-acre tract was thrown on the market and bought by Major William Page, the friend of Major Butler, and named by him Retreat. These were the four largest properties on St. Simon's.

John Couper was one of four sons of the Scotch pastor of Lochwinnoch, near Glasgow. At eighty, he wrote to his grandson, Hamilton Couper, "I was born on the 9th of March, 1759, at 1 oc. in the morning, in a dreadful snow-drift storm, and this is all I recollect on my coming into this best of all possible worlds. I believe I was an idle boy, preferring fishing and running about to my books, and so to get clear of me, I was transported from Scotland to Savannah, where I arrived 22nd of October, 1775."

At the age of sixteen John Couper and his best friend, James Hamilton, left Scotland, as he always said, "for the good of our country." He was indentured to Lundy and Company in Savannah, for the meagre wages of $125 a year and "found." When the Revolution started, this British firm moved to St. Augustine, and John Couper did not return to Georgia until it was over. He went first to Liberty County, where, in 1792, he married Rebecca, the daughter of Colonel James Maxwell, their oldest son, James Hamilton, being born in Sunbury in 1794.

He and his friend, James Hamilton, went into business together, were successful, and ultimately bought large tracts of land on the Altamaha for

planting purposes, making their homes meanwhile
on St. Simon's Island.

In 1804, Mr. Couper built a delightful house at
Cannon's Point, only a few yards from the river.
The ground floor, an English basement, was built
of tabby; the second, and the half story above it,
were of wood, all painted white with green blinds.
Surrounding the second story was a wide piazza
with a broad flight of steps leading to it, and on this
floor were the parlor, library, and dining room.
One of the pieces of furniture brought from Sunbury by Mrs. Couper was the "death chair," a large
winged armchair in which the Maxwell men met
death, like the Indian, face to face.   This unpleas-
ant piece of furniture may be still in the family,
but fortunately its history and itself have parted
company.

From the broad piazza at Cannon's Point, there
was a view across the marshes to the dark woods
of Little St. Simon's Island, beyond which lay the
great Atlantic.   In the brightness of day sea gulls
flew by on snowy wings.   In the silence of night
the soft lapping of the river soothed to slumber.
On three sides the house was surrounded by trees
and shrubs of every variety, for John Couper was
an ardent horticulturist and planted every flower
and tree that would grow in this balmy climate.

Figs and oranges, lemons, limes, guavas, pomegranates, and even olives and dates flourished at Cannon's Point, which has been called Georgia's first experimental station.

A letter from Thomas Jefferson gives an idea of John Couper's standing as a horticulturist.

To Monsieur Cathalan, Fils.
Consul des S. U. D. Amerique, à Marseilles.
Washington, *March 22*, '06.

Dear Sir,

You remember how anxious I was, when with you at Marseilles, to get the admirable olive of your canton transferred to my own country, and how much trouble you were so kind to take to effect it. It did not happen that any of those among whom the plants were distributed took up the plan with the enthusiasm necessary to give it success, and it has failed.

Mr. John Couper, of St. Simon's Island in Georgia, now proposes to undertake it, and being led to it by inclination, and a gentleman of property, in the most favorable situation, he will give the culture a fair trial, and I trust its favorable issue is beyond a doubt. He has been informed of the superior excellence of the olive of Marseilles, and knowing your friendly dispositions to our country I have taken the liberty of advising him to address himself to you, to put his commission into faithful hands. I ask the favor of you to give such aid to his operations as you can with convenience, and will deem it a great personal obligation rendered myself.

Accept for yourself and your respectable family my friendly salutations, and assurances of great esteem and consideration.

TH. JEFFERSON.

John Couper imported two hundred olive trees from Provence, and though five months on the voyage, most of the trees lived, and were planted at Cannon's Point. They grew well and produced from two to three hundred bottles of oil annually. In 1835, these trees were cut down by unprecedented cold, but shoots came up from the roots and the trees again bore olives.

In 1794, the Government searched the Atlantic Coast for timber for building vessels for the American navy, and found the live oak of the South adapted to this purpose. A quantity of timber was cut on St. Simon's and loaded for the North at Gascoigne's Bluff. Mr. Couper cut the stern post of the *Constitution* from a great oak which stood in his garden, and afterwards put an iron band around the stump, on which was inscribed, "U. S. Frigate, Constitution, 1794." A half century later, when the *Constitution* was docked for repairs in 1849, the Honorable Thomas Butler King, at that time Chairman of the Naval Committee, was presented with a vase carved from her timbers. So the oak that had grown at the north end of St. Simon's returned, after perils of storm and battle, to Retreat, at the south end of the island.

Cannon's Point was a resort for all who needed help or sought pleasure. Visitors have been known to stay, not for days or months, but for years, and a young couple who came to spend their honeymoon stayed until their second child was born. It seemed as though no one could visit Georgia without partaking of Mr. Couper's hospitality. A mine of wit and good humor, he was a delightful host, and his conversation and table talk, especially of Revolutionary days, were most entertaining. Always easy-going and light-hearted, he writes to a brother in Scotland: —

My wife has just disturbed me in a fever — unexpected company have dropped in, near dinner. Some lamb killed two days ago is *sower*. We have received no beef. (Wed. is beef day.) Our fisherman has returned with bad luck — it blows too hard — It is too late to kill poultry — so bacon and eggs. We may starve to-day, and tomorrow roll in plenty. Terrapin and sheep-head — not sheeps' head — We are Christians, taking no care for the morrow.

In addition to Cannon's Point, John Couper owned Long Island, east of St. Simon's, which he used as a pasture for his cattle. Fanny Kemble described it in 1839 as "a small green screen of wilderness that interposes between St. Simon's and the Atlantic. A wild little sand heap covered with thick forest growth, beyond which is the desolate beach and the boundless ocean."

Mr. Couper amassed what was at one time a large fortune, but no fortune could withstand his lavish hospitality, combined with losses from storms, crop failures, and other disasters, and later on he was obliged to sell the greater part of his interests to his partner, James Hamilton.

Like all Southern gentlemen of his time, Mr. Couper was interested in public affairs, and in 1796 was a member of the state legislature and aided in defeating the Yazoo Fraud. In 1798, he represented Glynn County and was in the convention that framed the Constitution. He was looked upon as a fine type of integrity, kindliness, and genial humor, and a younger generation remembered him with affection and pleasure.

Pierce Butler came of a fine old English family,

The Shell Road to Frederica, St. Simon's Island

and at the outbreak of the Revolution was an officer in the British army. Having married an heiress of the Middleton family (and to be a Middelton in South Carolina was like being a Hapsburg in Austria), he resigned his commission and became an ardent supporter of the Colonies. He was an associate in framing the Constitution, and a colaborer with Washington, Jefferson, Madison, and Franklin. He was an especial object of animosity to the English officers who attacked the Georgia coast, and sent troops ashore to carry off the Negroes and incite them to rise against their masters.

More than six hundred slaves called Major Butler "Master." These were equally divided between his rice place in McIntosh County, Butler's Island, at the mouth of the Altamaha, and his cotton plantation, Hampton Point. Because of his military training, Major Butler believed in the necessity for discipline in handling men, but he was absolutely just in the treatment of his slaves. They were not allowed to visit other plantations, with the exception of Cannon's Point, nor were other Negroes allowed to visit Hampton Point. His slaves were, however, allowed to row to Darien, the nearest market town, to sell their chickens, ducks, eggs, fish, and terrapin, and the thin wooden ware, tubs, buckets, and such, which they made by hand most skillfully from the cedars growing on their master's property. The Negroes of the Butler plantations were considered the most intelligent and thrifty in that community, although, owing to their isolation, their speech was hardly intelligible to outsiders.

Everything needed for the plantation was made at Hampton Point. There were a tannery, a shoemaking shop, a clothing manufactory; and almost every industry, including the making of furniture, was represented. No person on the place, however old and feeble, was allowed to be entirely idle. An old Negro woman, once coming to Major Butler, said, "Master, I am old. I can work no longer." "It is true," said Major Butler, and calling his head man, he said, "Flora is not to work, but get her a goose, give her a line, and every day she is to graze the goose for half an hour." And for ten years old Flora drove the goose to graze.

The discipline at Hampton Point was strict, but never harsh, a fact proved by the devoted, almost romantic attachment of every descendant of that slave population to all who have a drop of Butler blood in their veins.

In his social intercourse with the island families, Major Butler was stiff and ceremonious. He brought to his new home an overweening sense of his own importance and superiority to all of his island neighbors. He was, however, friendly with Mr. Couper, who said of him, "He was a good neighbor and citizen, and a just though strict master, considerate and humane to his people."

Major Butler lived in a species of feudal magnificence. The Butler mansion or "Big House," as it was called by his dependents, stood at the confluence of a bold creek and the river that ran in front of Hampton Point. On the land side it was approached by a fine avenue of live oaks. It was large and spacious, built of wood and tabby, and even in its decline when Fanny Kemble saw it, she describes it as "an imposing looking old dwelling." In the dairy was a capacious fish box or well, where the master's supply of fish was kept in clean salt water until required for the table.

Everything in the house and on the place was run by military rule. No one came to visit the Butlers without being met at the landing by a vidette, who ascertained his business, then escorted him to the mansion. A full corps of servants was always in attendance, whether the family was at home or abroad.

In the summer of 1804, Aaron Burr, "wishing to withdraw from public view" after his duel with

Alexander Hamilton, accepted an invitation from Major Butler to St. Simon's Island. He arrived in August, and it is said that he was serenaded by the island band, while the people all received him hospitably. Major Butler and his family soon after went North for the summer, and Burr occupied the house at Hampton Point alone.

He soon became acquainted with his nearest neighbor, Mr. John Couper, of whom he writes as follows to his beloved daughter, Theodosia, then Mrs. Alston of South Carolina.

HAMPTON, St. SIMON's, *August* 28 1804.

I am at the house of Major Butler, comfortably settled, a very agreeable family within half a mile. . . . My establishment consists of a house-keeper, cook and chamber-maid, seamstress and two footmen, two fishermen, and four boat-men always at my command. The laundry work is done outside. . . .

August 31*st* 1804.

Yesterday my neighbor Mr. Couper sent me an assortment of French wines, claret and sauternes, all excellent. Also an orange shrub, a delicious punch, and Madam Couper added sweetmeats and pickles sufficient to last at least twelve months. . . . The plantations of Butler and Couper are divided by a small creek. The cotton crop in this neighborhood has been entirely destroyed. The crop of

Mr. Couper was supposed to be worth a hundred thousand dollars. He will not get enough to pay one half of the expense of the plantation. Yet he laughs about it with good humour and without affectation. . . . Madame Couper is still young, tall, comely and well bred.

On another day, having dined and evidently dined well, his bright soul breaks out as follows: —

HAMPTON POINT, *Sep.* 1804.

MADAME: —

J' ai bien dîner, and J' ai fait mettre mon writing desk sur le table à dîner. What a scandalous thing to sit here all alone, drinking champagne, and yet (Madame, je bois à votre santé et à celle de Monsieur votre fils), and yet I say if champagne be that exhilarating cordial which (je bois à la santé de Madame Sumtare) can there ever be an occasion more appropriate (Mais buvons à la santé de mon hôte et bon ami Major Butler).

Sep. 3rd 1804.

You see me returned from Gaston's Bluff, now called Hamilton's Bluff, from a London merchant, partner of Mr. C.

In less than two weeks after this a terrible hurricane swept the island, which Aaron Burr described in the following letter: —

Sep. 12th 1804.

On Friday last hearing that Mr. Couper had returned home and was seriously ill, I took a small canoe with two boys and went to see him. He lay in a high fever. When about to return in the evening the wind had risen so that after an ineffectual attempt, I was obliged to give it up and remain at Mr. C's. In the morning the wind was still higher. It continued to rise, and by noon blew a gale from the north, which together with the swelling of the waters became alarming. From twelve to three several of the out-houses had been destroyed, and most of the trees about the house had been blown down. The house in which we were shook and rocked so much that Mr. C. began to express his apprehension for our safety. Before three part of the piazza was carried away, two or three of the windows bursted in, the house was inundated with water, and presently one of the chimneys fell. Mr. C. then commenced a retreat to a store house about fifty yards off, and we decamped, men, women and children. You may imagine in this scene of confusion many incidents to amuse one, if one had dared to be amused, in a moment of such anxiety. The house however did not blow down. The storm continued until four, and then very suddenly abated and in ten minutes was almost a calm. I seized the moment to return home. Before I quite got over, the gale rose from the south-east, and threatened new destruction. It lasted a great part of the night, but did not attain the volume of that from the north, yet it contrived to raise still higher the water which was the principal instrument of destruction. The flood was about seven feet above the height of an ordinary tide. This has been sufficient to inundate a great part of the coast, to destroy all the rice, to carry off most of the buildings which were in the low lands, and to destroy the lives of many blacks.

Major Butler's head man, who was named Morris, was a remarkable Negro. He had charge of the slaves who worked on a small island north of St. Simon's, to which they rowed every day. When Morris saw the storm coming he ordered the Negroes into the hurricane house, the only building on the island. They were frantic to return to their homes on St. Simon's, but he drove them in with the lash, and they were hardly secured before the storm broke, one of the worst ever known on the Southern coast. Not a life was lost of these Butler Negroes, while over a hundred were drowned on Broughton Island, north of St. Simon's.

As a reward for his admirable conduct, Major Butler offered Morris his freedom, but having a wife and children on the island, he refused it. His master then gave him a considerable sum of money, and a silver goblet on which was engraved the following inscription: —

TO MORRIS

FROM

P. BUTLER

FOR HIS FAITHFUL, JUDICIOUS AND SPIRITED
CONDUCT IN THE HURRICANE OF SEPTEM-
BER 8TH, 1804, WHEREBY THE LIVES
OF MORE THAN 100 PERSONS
WERE, BY DIVINE PER-
MISSION, SAVED

This goblet passed to his grandson Morris, a worthy descendant, who showed it in 1870 to Mrs. Leigh, the great-granddaughter of Major Butler.

The name "Aaron Burr" was cut on one of the windowpanes at Cannon's Point, and was fondly supposed to have been cut by Burr himself. James Maxwell Couper, the grandson of old John, who inherited his delightful sense of humor, confessed that it had been cut by his first cousin, Fannie Fraser, with her diamond ring.

Major Butler and his family lived at Hampton Point from 1795 to 1815, staying there only during the winter and spending the summers in South Carolina or Philadelphia. After the death of his wife,

Major Butler moved to Philadelphia to live, where he built one of the finest houses to be seen at that time in the Quaker city.

Major Butler and Major Page were two of the first to plant sea-island cotton, and when the first crop was sent from Hampton Point to Liverpool, it was worth in the cotton market half a guinea a pound. The manager of this estate, Mr. Roswell King of New England, with his son had charge of Hampton Point for thirty years, and lived to see sea-island cotton go down, in 1839, to less than a shilling a pound. Yet in spite of the decline in price, cotton remained the staple crop of St. Simon's.

Hamilton and Retreat, the two other large properties on the island, were both delightful places. Of the former Fanny Kemble wrote, as late as 1839, "Hamilton is by far the finest estate on St. Simon's Island. The whole appearance of the place struck me very much, the situation of the house, the noble water prospect it commanded, the magnificent old oaks, and its splendid hedge of Yucca Gloriosa." In spite of its attractiveness, James Hamilton ultimately left his island home and, like Major Butler, went to Philadelphia to live, where he married a Miss Janet Wilson, their only child being a daughter.

Retreat was just below Hamilton on the southwest point of the island, within sight of the glorious Atlantic, and for almost a century, first as the home of the Pages, and afterwards as that of the Kings, it remained one of the most hospitable and delightful homes on St. Simon's.

The rest of the island was divided into smaller places, there being fourteen homesteads in all. Below Hampton Point were Pike's Bluff and West Point, the homes of Dr. Thomas Hazzard and of his brother, Colonel William Hazzard. The picturesque ruins of the tabby slave quarters, and of their little church are still in existence at West Point. A few families still lived at Frederica, but most of the islanders, like their progenitors, preferred to live on their country estates.

On the eastern side of the island, below Cannon's Point, were Long View, Lawrence, Oatlands, St. Clair, and the Village. Kelvyn Grove was farther down on this side, while Harrington Hall and Mulberry Grove were in the interior of the island.

At Longview lived Mrs. McNish with her charming daughter, who afterwards became Mrs. Leighton Hazelhurst. At Lawrence was Captain John Fraser, a half-pay British officer. At Oatlands was Dr. Grant, a Northern man who had come to St. Simon's to practise medicine. At St. Clair were the Alexander Wyllys, who in 1809 leased this place from the lady who was known as Mrs. Rainbow McIntosh.

The Village had been sold by the Moravians, when they left St. Simon's, to George Baillie, who sold it in turn to his uncle, Captain Wylly, who moved his family there in 1812. St. Clair then became the home of Dr. William Fraser, a retired British surgeon and brother of Captain Fraser.

Alexander Campbell Wylly, whose father had come from Belfast, Ireland, to Savannah, Georgia, was born in that city in 1759, had been educated at Oxford, and remained loyal to Great Britain when the Revolution began. He became a captain in the British army, crossed the St. Mary's with General Prevost, and marched with him to Savannah. His grandson, Charles Wylly, says, "He was undeservedly censured for harshness and cruelty in the execution of orders transmitted from the headquarters of General Prevost, the Commander in Chief." After the Revolution, realizing that feeling would be against him, he went to the Bahamas to live. There he was made Governor of New Providence, fell in love with Margaret Armstrong, a lovely girl he saw walking on the seashore, and married her.

In the course of time the governor received a

letter from his friend Mr. Gladstone, — father of the great statesman, — telling him of the movement in England to free the slaves in the Colonies. Mr. Gladstone himself was the owner of many hundreds of slaves in the Barbados and British Guiana. Captain Wylly was outraged. "What!" he cried, "Shall a government for whom I fought against my own kin and dearest friends, for adherence to which my father, mother, brother and myself were banished from Georgia; a government in whose service I fought from the Altamaha to Yorktown; shall this government now rob me of what is my own? Before I will submit to such injustice, I will return to Savannah, Georgia, where I was born." His brother William, chief justice of Trinidad, tried in vain to dissuade him, and in 1807 Captain Wylly moved back with his family to the States.

The Wyllys stayed first on Jekyl Island, which was owned by the Du Bignons, and here three of their children were born. In 1810 they moved up to St. Simon's and leased the substantial tabby house at St. Clair, which had been built by Captain James McKay. Their youngest child, Caroline Georgia Wylly, was born in this house in 1811, and the next year they moved to the Village, where Captain and Mrs. Wylly spent the rest of their lives.

Harrington Hall and Mulberry Grove, three miles below it, were owned by the descendants of Captain Raymond Demaré. The Raymond *Demere* of this day lived at Mulberry Grove with his younger sons, while Paul and John, the older ones, lived at Harrington Hall.

In 1805, the lighthouse on the south end of the island was built by James Gould, a young engineer from New England. He had come down to Florida on a government contract for timber, and settled on the St. Mary's River. In an Indian uprising his house was burned, and hearing of the plan to build a lighthouse on St. Simon's, he applied for the contract. This beautiful lighthouse was built almost entirely of materials from the old walls and fortifications of Frederica. James Gould found the island so attractive that he decided to make it his home, and, buying from the Commissioner of Confiscated Estates a tract of land known as the John Graham–St. Clair tract, he built a house, which he called Rosemount, and moved with his family to St. Simon's. This place was in the interior between the two Demere estates, and was well named, as it was noted for its wonderfully beautiful roses.

The last place on the island was Kelvyn Grove, which bordered the old battlefield of Bloody Marsh.

The land was originally granted to William McIntosh, and had been bought by Thomas Cater. The house was a large and substantial one, built of brick and tabby, and stood in its dark setting of trees until recent times, when it was destroyed by fire. Here Thomas Cater lived with his young and attractive wife, who had been Elizabeth Franklin, and here an awful tragedy took place.

A handsome overseer won the heart of Elizabeth Cater, and plotted to murder her husband. On the night of the dreadful deed old Benbow, Thomas Cater's "man," saw his mistress and the murderer consorting, and feeling that little Benjamin, the only child, was in danger of his life, he took the boy on his back and made his way through the woods to Major Page at Retreat.

The guilty pair fled from the island and were heard of no more, and the courts made Major Page the guardian of Benjamin Franklin Cater. He had the boy well educated, sending him finally to Yale, and managed his property so well that when he became a man he was able to take his proper place on St. Simon's as the master of Kelvyn Grove.

These men now established on St. Simon's belonged to a distinctive class. They were men of education, often of travel and wide experience. To a certain extent they were overbearing in opinion, for the habit of command necessitated by their position brought with it a dogmatism not open to argument. In speech and manner, however, they exhibited a constant courtesy to equal and inferior, and were distinguished by a universal desire for the upbuilding of their country and a love of the Union.

VI

SAPELO

JAMES SPALDING died in 1794, leaving to his only son, Thomas, $20,000 — all that remained of his former large estate. Thomas was studying law at the time in the office of Judge Gibbons of Savannah, and was admitted to the bar in the following year at the age of twenty-one. Before he was twenty-four he became engaged to Miss Sarah Leake, of Belleville, McIntosh County, a great beauty who was endowed with many gifts of mind and heart.

Thomas Spalding built on his St. Simon's estate, which was called Orange Grove, a unique house for his bride. It was low to the ground on account of hurricanes, and every timber in it was of squared live oak, held together by hand-wrought pegs. On each side of the great kitchen chimney was a niche — one to hold a cask of Madeira, the other a thirty-gallon puncheon of brandy. As the fire in the kitchen burned perpetually, the aging of the wine and brandy was hastened, and the quality improved.

Thomas Spalding did not bring his bride to St. Simon's, however, but sailed instead for Scotland, and his Orange Grove property was sold to Major Page.

The father of Major Page was Thomas Page of Page's Point, Prince William Parish, South Carolina. When the Revolution began, Thomas Page remained loyal to Great Britain, but when he died soon after, his son William, though only sixteen, joined the Rebel forces under Marion, and remained in the service until the end of the war. He married his cousin, Hannah Timmons, and their early life together was spent in the dreadful days of civil war, when no man was safe from a Tory neighbor. One of Major Page's granddaughters wrote, "I have seen a big wooden chest, in which Mother told us her father lay concealed, while the Tories searched the house for him."

After the Revolution, as the house at Page's Point had been destroyed by fire, Major Page decided to move to Georgia, and purchased a plantation in Bryan County. This place was on the Medway River, and proved so unhealthy for his children that he decided to move again. About this time his friend Major Butler was moving from South Carolina to Georgia, and he helped him bring down his large number of Negroes to St. Simon's

Island. Major Page was so pleased with the place that he decided to settle there himself, and, buying the Spalding property, he changed its name to Retreat.

When Thomas Spalding arrived in Scotland with his beautiful wife, he communicated with the firm of Messrs. Simpson in London and Edinburgh, was received kindly by them, and assured of their interest in the son of a valued friend, whose loss of wealth they ascribed to his loyalty to the crown. These gentlemen placed young Spalding in a way to better his fortune, and he did not return to America for five years.

Those were the days when inherited integrity and personal character were recognized in the marts of trade as collaterals to be honored by banks and money lenders. After four years of increasing approval, Mr. Simpson said to Thomas Spalding, "In your father's lifetime our firm made large sums of money through our connection with him. We are too old to resume our American transactions, but, knowing the opportunities offered there, we are prepared to lend you $50,000 at 3½ per cent, on your own personal note, due in ten years." Thomas Spalding accepted the generous offer, and with funds thus provided arrived in Savannah early in the year 1802.

His first concern was to provide a home for his wife and the four children who had been born in Scotland. He had sold all of his property on St. Simon's, excepting Frederica, and hearing that the south end of Sapelo was for sale, he decided to buy four thousand acres there.

In 1788, the island of Sapelo had been bought by five French gentlemen — Messieurs De Mousset, De la Chappeldelaine, Grande de Marlet, Poulain du Bignon, and De Bœufeillet. Three of these gentlemen made their homes on the island, while the others were, in all likelihood, mere investors. The Bœufeillets and Chappeldelaines were from distinguished French families, so were naturally royalists. Disapproving of the radical tendencies of the day, they determined to leave France and make their homes elsewhere. Owing to dissensions, the copartnership was dissolved in 1802, De Bœufeillet alone remaining, while the four other Frenchmen became the owners of Jekyl Island.

The place at the north end, belonging to Grande de Marlet, was resold to the Marquis de Montalet, a French nobleman who had fled from St. Domingo, where every member of his family had been massacred by the blacks. He called his new home Le Châtelet, which by Negro mispronunciation — Chaclet — was finally debased to Chocolate.

The Marquis de Montalet, whom his neighbors described as "a dear, good old gentleman," devoted himself to the cultivation of his flowers and fruits, and to the training of his Negro cook, Cupidon, whom he declared to be a genius and the equal of Vatel. When he considered that Cupid had reached perfection, he placed the *cordon bleu* above his kitchen door.

The old Marquis and his companion, the Chevalier de la Horne, lived a quiet life, only being visited now and then by the Abbé Karle from Savannah. Accompanied by one friend or the other, the old French gentleman would be seen walking beneath the oaks, leading a pig in leash. Quaint figures the Marquis and the Chevalier must have been, in their broad-skirted coats and knee breeches, as they earnestly scrutinized the pig's search for acorns and other food. They treasured the hope that in this way truffles might be found. The Chevalier was encouraging. "I think, Alphonse, we will one day find them," he would say; and the Marquis would reply, "I would that we might, for the eating of truffles makes men more gay and women more tender, and in this country we need them. Mon Dieu!"

When Thomas Spalding moved to Sapelo, he built a temporary home for his family, then looked

around for the industrial power he needed to clear
the forests and prepare the land for planting. He
was the great-grandson of John Morh McIntosh,
the author of the New Inverness protest against
the introduction of slaves into Georgia, and he had
not forgotten its prophetic closing clause. But
Negro labor was indispensable, his environment
justified slavery, and he excused himself by saying,
"They shall be more serfs than slaves on my land.
I shall civilize them, and better their condition."
He kept his word, being a kind and indulgent master. The tasks of his slaves were comparatively
light, they had many privileges, and no slave
was ever sold from his place. But the penalty was
incurred, and the "scourge" was visited on his descendants.

Mr. Spalding bought some of his slaves in
Charleston, some in the West Indies, selecting certain hands trained for the management and guidance of such raw labor. The government was at
this time buying live-oak timber for the building
of ships, and he contracted to supply the timber,
and in this way cleared his lands. Fields were
drained and fenced by piling the limbs of the oaks
around them. On favorable spots villages of huts
were built, the houses being plastered inside and
out, and each village was in charge of a head man

or driver. Mr. Spalding was among the first to plant cotton, and he also introduced cane and the manufacture of sugar into Georgia.

No slave was bought on the South End plantation after 1810, and no slave was ever sold during the lifetime of the master. The natural increase was phenomenal. In the plantation books of 1840–1851, for 400 souls the birth rate was 60, 70, and 80, while the death rate was 5, 6, and 7. Several causes contributed to this result—chiefly the youth and equality in number of the sexes. Slave vessels seldom shipped "merchandise" younger than fifteen, or older than twenty-four. Then there were the easy hours of labor, and the plentiful supply of food.

On the Georgia coast slaves were seldom bought in a larger number than fifty at a time, the sexes being equal. Purchased usually in Charleston, they would be transferred at once to the plantation. Here would be found a number of men and women acquired in former years, sometimes of the same race and tribe, speaking the same dialect, or at least able to make themselves understood. To one of these would be given ten men, with the right to issue their food. To a woman with the same gifts—fluency of speech and ability to command —ten women would be assigned. To a third and

Architect's Drawing of the Old South-end House on Sapelo

fourth, the boys and girls. The slaves' education was now started, their reward being an abundance of good food. No work was expected of them at first. After a training of from three to five months they were assigned to work, usually beginning with such manual labor as the gathering of shells, the mixing of lime for concrete, the making of mortar beds, and the pouring of the tabby into the building moulds. In twelve months the slave was usually "tamed," as it was called, and had acquired some knowledge of the English language. Not until then did his master take notice of his individual qualities and assign him to the duty for which he was best fitted.

The second year usually found the new slave with a gang of thirty, assigned to regular labor in the fields. One third of the gang would be men and women of his own race, who had graduated years before from the school he was now entering. The driver of each gang was always near to teach or command, and by the end of the year the new slave had learned many things. He rose when the conch blew in the morning, came and went when told to do so, stood still when a white man spoke to him, and used his hoe in the proper manner. By the end of the second year, "Jack, New Negro," which marked his place on the plantation books, would be changed to "Jack, African born," which meant an immense change in his status.

No one living can imagine with what ease and freedom from danger was the African of 1779 to 1808 trained into the most inefficient, but the most easily managed laborer in the world.

A race docile, obedient, and affectionate, especially to the youth of a family, identifying itself with the wealth and standing of its owners, and loyal to the very name. Possessed of the strongest local attachments, the African slaves were given by Providence a calm and philosophic power to accept the most radical changes in life without comment, complaint, or even show of feeling. It was as though, deep in their hearts, fatalism was the creed of their race. At this time in the history of the South both races made an honest effort to "do their duty in that state of life to which it had pleased God to call them." And it was the honest opinion of one who knew whereof he spoke that "in this earliest stage of plantation life was found the happiest form of peasant life the world could show."

The Negroes took a curious pride in belonging to such and such a family, and frequently called themselves by what to them was an all but tribal name. Their language was a mixture of African and English, and, uncouth as it was in sound, it had the merit of strength and vitality. Often as a language becomes more refined, it loses its pristine power. The Gulla spoken by the Coast Negroes was almost unintelligible to outsiders, but when understood was original, picturesque, and powerful. On every plantation, among both field and house servants, would be found one or two recognized story-tellers, who possessed real dramatic talent. Every white Southern child of the years gone by has thrilled over the "true and true" stories of Brer Rabbit.

That the Negroes were loyal to their masters was proved by repeated instances. Mr. Spalding's head man, Bu Allah, was of a superior African race, a man of unusual intelligence and character. He and all the members of his family were tall, well made, and had fine features. They were Mohammedans, and three times a day, Bi-lal-y, as he was called, spread his sheepskin prayer rug, knelt, and, turning to the East, prayed to Allah. This family spoke English, but among themselves used a language which no one else understood, and Bu Allah kept the plantation acts in Arabic. He always wore a cap which resembled a Turkish fez, and the whole family held themselves aloof from the other Africans, as though conscious of their superiority. Bu Allah was implicitly obeyed by the four hundred Negroes, who answered proudly when questioned, "We are Spalding Negroes."

Thomas Spalding had perfect confidence in the loyalty of his slaves, and when in 1813 a British fleet lay off Sapelo Island, he applied to the Governor for arms, and, receiving eighty muskets, armed and drilled his Negroes. As the water was not deep around the island, only a boat attack was possible, and he said that if that was attempted, he and Bu Allah would give a good account of the enemy. "I will answer for every Negro of the true faith," said Bu Allah, "but not for the *Christian dogs* you own." No attack was made on Sapelo, though on St. Simon's over three hundred slaves were carried off, so large a number of those belonging to Mr. John Couper that it was one of the causes of his financial reverses.

Bu Allah, who was the father of twelve sons and seven daughters, lived to be a very old man. When he died, over eighty years of age, his Koran and prayer rug were buried with him.

When the land on the South End of Sapelo had been cleared and planted in cotton, corn, and cane, Thomas Spalding turned his attention to the building of what was to be known as the South End

home. The work was done under the direction of
Mr. Roswell King, Major Butler's manager, by
trained Negro mechanics, and so well was the house
built that on its foundations the present beautiful South End home of the Howard Coffins was
erected.

The original house was built of tabby, the walls
being three feet thick. The four reception rooms
were each twenty-six by thirty-two feet, the bed-
rooms above of corresponding size. The south
room, looking out on the ocean, was used as a library, and was filled with the books Thomas Spalding had begun collecting in Edinburgh. His
library was one of the largest and best selected in
the South, but as Mr. Spalding lent his books to
any and every one, many were lost as the years
went by, and many sets were broken.

Mr. Spalding cared nothing for art, and there
were few pictures on the walls, with the exception
of a set of steel engravings of Le Brun's master-
pieces, "The Crossing of the Grannicus" having
the place of honor over the sideboard in the dining
room. No bric-a-brac adorned the rooms besides
the four female figures in the parlor, holding lamps
in their outstretched hands, and the beautiful marble bust of Napoleon, which had been taken from

life on his return from his first Italian campaign.

Thomas Spalding was a stern, yet tender, loving, and generous man, giving of his abundance to all except himself, and a most considerate master. His slaves had a task each day, which, when completed, gave them the remaining hours to do with as they pleased. They were allowed to raise hogs and poultry, and the more privileged families were permitted to own cattle and horses. Mr. Spalding's system created among his slaves a self-reliance and an ability to think for themselves. It was exactly the opposite of the military discipline of Major Butler, but, strange to say, the two contrasting systems produced the same unswerving loyalty to the master.

There was constant intercourse between the islands and the mainland of the Georgia coast, and staunch friendships were formed where interests were the same. Thomas Spalding and John Couper were warm friends, though absolutely different in temperament and tastes. Mr. Spalding disapproved sternly of dancing and card playing, disliked music, and had no taste for art. Above all he had no sense of humor, which was John Couper's most delightful gift. Mr. Spalding's sense of personal honor was, however, acute, and in 1802

he wrote his friend the following remarkable
letter: —

JOHN COUPER.
CANNON'S POINT,
ST. SIMON'S ISLAND.

MY DEAR FRIEND:

I write you to-day to ask you the personal favor
which a gentleman has only the right to ask of one
whom he esteems as his nearest and best friend.
I write you to come over and bring your duelling
pistols.   Mine are so rusted from disuse and salt
air, that the flint does not draw spark from the
steel.

The cause of my call is this.   It has as you know
been lately shown and proved by the arrival of Dr.
—— of Wilmington, Delaware, that that rascally
cousin of mine,——, was eight years ago married
to the Doctor's sister of the same state.   That the
marriage was a secret one, and only has now been
divulged by the peremptory call of Dr. —— on
—— to acknowledge and receive his sister as
his wife and equal, which has been acceded to,
and that the two are now living in the home in
Camden County, and are most happily placed I
am told.

It immediately occurred to me that this cousin
had presumed in 1794, before I had obtained Miss
Leake's favor, to offer himself as a suitor for her
hand.   I have subtracted 7 years from 1802, and

it leaves 1795, which was the year of my own marriage.   Therefore, while a married man, he had
presumed to offer himself to a lady as a suitor of
marriage.   Nothing remains but for me to shoot
him.   Come over, and I shall furnish you with a
good boat, and hands to take you to Camden
County.

Yours sincerely and truly,

THOMAS SPALDING.

One can hear John Couper shout as he read the
words, "Nothing remains but for me to shoot him,"
and pictured to himself the astonishment of——,
now so "happily placed" with his wife in Camden
County.   Whether he accepted the invitation to
Sapelo is not known, but at any rate he did not
take over his dueling pistols.   The affair was "ar-
ranged," and no duel took place.

Every Southern gentleman had his dueling pistols as a matter of course, neatly fitted in a felt-
lined mahogany box, with his initials engraved on a
plate on the top.   The dueling pistol was the su-
preme court to which all personal difficulties were
referred, and the settlement was short and decisive.
General Charles Floyd, before whom many of these
cases were adjudged, called himself the Peace
Maker, "for," said he, "I have settled more dis-
putes than any Judge in Georgia, either by amiable

reconciliation, or by the *removal* of one or both of the disputants."

The wife whose honor Mr. Spalding was so quick to defend was worthy of his devotion and reverence. It was said of her by Charles Cotesworth Pinckney of Charleston, "Mrs. Spalding, sir, would grace a court or sweeten a dairy." Instead of the life of indolent ease which the Southern mistress was supposed to lead, her own was one of ceaseless activity. At nine in the morning the plantation nurse arrived with a list or "tally" of the sick. The serious cases were visited and a physician summoned if necessary. Personal interviews followed with the cook, butcher, and fisherman. At twelve the three plantation seamstresses arrived with their baskets of completed garments, which had to be checked up and assigned to the slaves. It was not until two o'clock that Mrs. Spalding had a brief rest, for there were countless other duties in connection with her household. With a growing family — she had sixteen children in all, though only seven reached maturity — nothing but the presence of that "gift of the Gods," the Southern "Mauma," could render life less than a burden.

The master led quite as busy a life. Mr. Spalding rose at half-past seven and rode over the place until breakfast. Immediately afterward he started out again, visiting the different Negro settlements and attending to all plantation affairs. If he met any friend or neighbor on his way, that friend was always asked to dinner. At half after four this meal was served to a number unknown to the mistress until they assembled at table. One of his daughters said she never remembered sitting down to dinner with less than twenty-four!

For Mrs. Spalding life was a perpetual house party. Servants she had in numbers, but, excepting perhaps a butler or head housemaid, they were often idle and incompetent, and needed her constant supervision. Her servants were all devoted to her, and to her slaves, some of them hardly reclaimed Africans, she was a saint, almost a deity.

During the lifetime of the Spaldings there was a charming social life on Sapelo. The De Bœufeillets, with true Gallic vivacity, made ceremonious visits, and entertained when Madame Cottineau and her brother the Abbé Karle came from Savannah in summer. At the Châtelet the old Marquis and Major Horne welcomed all visitors cordially.

The two elderly French gentlemen led a different life from that of their Southern neighbors.

No ambition to accumulate wealth stirred their souls. They had played their part in the drama of life, and now, retired from the stage, they awaited the fall of the curtain. Their faithful colored servants looked after their wants — Cupidon, his wife Venus, their son Hercules, and his wife Ceres. Hercules, besides being gardener, was hunter and fisherman, and kept the table bountifully supplied with fish and game. In the carelessly cultivated fields, some dozens of slaves worked a little, idled more, and produced a sufficiency of food for themselves, and sometimes a thousand dollars' worth of cotton, enough for the purchase of coffee, flour, sugar, a few luxuries, and some good wine and brandy.

In the sitting room of Le Châtelet, a shelf held the volumes of Racine, Rousseau, Voltaire, Molière, and Brillat-Savarin's great work, *The Physiology of Taste*. It was probably after the perusal of this immortal volume that the Marquis de Montalet conceived the idea of civilizing the Americans through a diet of truffles.

When Mr. Couper decided to plant olives at Cannon's Point, he paid a visit to the old Marquis to consult him on the subject. He was courteously received, and of course invited to dinner. Cupidon was informed that Mr. Couper was an epicure, so he prepared a special repast. A *purée* of artichokes, with two onions mashed into the cream, the bottom of the tureen rubbed with a sliced garlic, was served boiling hot. This was followed by prawn. From the head of each prawn, Cupidon had taken the fat, and mixed it with the sauce "Cupidon-Montalet," which his master and himself had composed. Next came a *poularde,* fried in olive oil and masked in sweet cream.

Cupidon stood at the dining-room door, and his heart swelled when he saw Mr. Couper, after the first mouthful, lift his eyes to heaven. He said nothing, but after dinner, when the Marquis and the Major were playing dominos as they sipped their wine, "the big gentleman" knocked at the kitchen door. "I wish to thank you, Cupidon," he said, "for to-day's great pleasure. Such cooking is *the same as prayer.* If you ever have a day or week of your own, I wish you would come down to Cannon's Point on St. Simon's Island, and instruct my boy, Sans Foix."

Cupidon remembered and afterwards profited by these words.

In 1811, the lights still burned at Le Châtelet, showing the shadows of the two old men bending over the last copy of *Le Moniteur,* which told of the victories of the *scélérat* Napoleon. Above the mantel were their two rapiers, crossed, point up, and they lifted their eyes reverently to the white cockade pinned on them. They, at least, were true to the lilies of Bourbon.

But before 1824 the doors were closed and the blinds drawn at Le Châtelet. The loyal heart and gentle soul of the Chevalier de la Horne were the first to be summoned to the final roll call. The Marquis did not long survive him. Cupidon, Venus, and Hercules ministered faithfully to his few wants, and were freed by his last will and testament. Cupidon said to a Spalding lad of fourteen, who had ridden up to inquire, "Master never held up after Mass Armand's death. When he took down the sword to put in his coffin, he left his own on the wall, but turned it point down." (The fencer's signal that the combat is over.) "I did my best to prepare the little dishes he liked. But when I took in the *poulet à la marengo,* with mushrooms, he would only taste it and say, 'Thank you, Cupid. It is superb. You improve wonderfully.' On the last day, and it was full ebb tide, he laid a long while without speaking, his eyes looking far away. I saw his lips move, and leaned over to hear. 'Armand,' he said, 'we need hunt the truffles no more, for here all are gentle and tender.' Then he turned his face to the wall, and was gone."

He had lived "in simpleness, and gentleness and honor and clean mirth." He had done his work, had held his peace, and had no fear of death.

It was in the spring of the year 1822 that an elderly gentleman, a Mr. Wambazee of Bruro Neck, heir and executor to the Marquis de Montalet, came in his six-oared boat to the Châtelet. Mr. Wambazee was a Belgian by birth, short, florid, and fat. He walked through the lovely garden without plucking bud or blossom, unconscious of the sweet perfume of Devoniensis and Lady Bankshire, and gave Cupidon, Venus, and Hercules their letters of manumission. Then, summoning the remaining slaves, he jotted down in a memorandum book names, apparent ages, and attributes. Mr. Wambazee would take luncheon, and Cupidon hastily prepared the meal. "Vene, a chicken," he had called. "One not over six weeks old. To be broiled with mushrooms. A salad from the white hearts of the best lettuce — only tarragon vinegar to be used. A bottle of claret of the Blue Seal, and wafers." When he rose from the table, it was with a sigh that Mr. Wambazee looked at the white-capped figure in the doorway. "Cupid," he said, "I am sorry your master freed you in his will.

I never would have parted with you." And then,
with a few words of farewell, Mr. Wambazee
moved down the garden, and took his way to Savannah. That night he would sleep at St. Catherine's, the next at Green Island, and on the third he
would reach Savannah. And as soon as the
stranger had gone, Cupidon said, "Now, Herk,
us three will go to Cannon's Point. You will tend
the olives, for which Mr. Couper will pay you
$6.00 a month with 'lowance and clothes. Vene
will see to the poultry yard, and I will just cook,
and teach Sans Fox and 'zort." His plan was
carried out, and on St. Simon's, Cupidon trained
Sans Foix to excel himself, and made of French
Davy and Abraham Fire-All, who belonged to the
Wyllys and Hamilton Coupers, two other famous
chefs.

And so farewell to the Châtelet, with its memories of courtesy, gentle breeding, and high courage,
for does it not require a brave heart to face the
world, aged, poor, wifeless, and childless, and yet
to smile? Farewell to the fragrance of sweet
olive and heliotrope. The idyllic days have passed,
and the dawn of materialism is at hand. The
Châtelet was sold by Mr. Wambazee to Captain
Swarbreck, a Dane, who had been a slave trader,
but was naturally a kindly man and good to his

dependents. He replaced all of the buildings, including the slaves' quarters, with solid tabby structures, and lived at the Châtelet until the early thirties, when he in turn sold it to a Northerner, Dr. Rogers. Over his barn Dr. Rogers placed a slab of marble from the grave of the old Marquis, and for years there was nothing to mark the lonely grave on High Point as de Montalet's save tradition. In the tidal wave of 1898, the sea encroached, tore open the grave, and scattered the bones upon the shore.

At intervals the Georgia coast has been swept by hurricanes. That of 1824 was one of the most terrific, and Sapelo was in its very vortex. The island was in part overflowed, and heavy losses were incurred by the drowning of horses, cattle, and other stock. Terror reigned in the great Spalding house at the South End, for while those in the solid, flat-roofed house were comparatively safe, the utmost anxiety was felt for the father, who had left the island the day before, and for the hundreds of slaves, who lived on lower ground in the frailest of structures. All night long the storm raged. Shutters were torn off and windows blown in, and the entire house deluged with rain, but at dawn there came a cessation, and a runner from the Barn Creek settlement brought the good news that all was well. Bu Allah had, the day before, given orders to each of the drivers to take every man, woman, and child into the cotton and sugar houses, and in these two-storied substantial buildings not a life was lost. By nine o'clock in the morning, Mr. Spalding returned. Such was his determination that he would have been down the night before, but his prudent Negro oarsmen had run away and hidden themselves.

At twelve o'clock a melancholy procession appeared. The overseer, supporting his wife, who was carrying her baby, was followed by the blind old father mounted on a horse, which was led by Selina, a colored woman. Their oldest child, a little girl, had been drowned the night before. Terrified by the violence of the storm, the family had abandoned their house in an effort to reach higher ground. Attempting to cross a gully, which had now become a roaring torrent, they had lost their footing and been swept against the roots of an uprooted tree. In the struggle the child had been torn from the mother's grasp and disappeared without a cry, swallowed in the darkness. Clinging to the roots, the family had spent a terrible night, and when the dawn came they saw that their house was intact. Selina and her son had stayed in it, and they, as well as the horse in its stall, were uninjured. Rescued from their perilous position, the little party made its sorrowful way to the great house at the South End. Here they were taken in, comforted, fed, and put to bed, although inside the house all was wrack and ruin. But a great thanksgiving went up to the Divine Mercy that had spared the lives of the family.

As the years went on Thomas Spalding acquired wealth, and by 1843 almost the whole of Sapelo was in his hands. Each year increased his importance in county and state. After the War of 1812 he was sent to Bermuda to negotiate terms of payment for the slaves and other property which had been taken by the British from the Georgia coast. With his friend, John Couper, he helped frame the constitution of his state, and was in the legislature for many years. He served two terms in Congress, and like many of his compeers was a strong Union man.

Like most human beings, Thomas Spalding was inconsistent. Absolute in his opinions, he required submission to them in others. Dominant for years over all the island, he was domineering even to his children, and, violating all custom, became in the end a law unto himself.

VII

THE EDEN OF GEORGIA

In the first quarter of the nineteenth century we find on St. Simon's Island a society in which are numbered the son of a great English family, Major Butler; a gentleman of Scotch birth, Mr. John Couper; an Oxford graduate, Mr. George Baillie; an officer of the Revolution, Major Page; and a number of officers of the British army.

Captain Alexander Wylly has already been spoken of. Lieutenant Colonel Wardrobe had served with Napier and Wellington, in India and the Peninsular, and now, broken in health, had retired on half pay, to spend the closing years of a stirring life on quiet St. Simon's. He had married Eliza Baillie, the first cousin of Captain Wylly. John Fraser, a retired British captain, had seen service with Sir John Moore and borne himself bravely at Corunna. He had married Ann, the oldest daughter of Mr. John Couper, and they were at this time living at Lawrence, a mile south of Cannon's Point. His brother, Dr. William

Fraser, had been surgeon in chief to the East India forces under his friend Warren Hastings, had for many years resided in Calcutta, and spoke Hindustani like a native. He had married Frances, the fourth daughter of Captain Wylly, and later removed to Darien. George Baillie, cynic and wit, was the nephew of Captain Wylly, and the most polished man in four counties. Now a widower, he was living alone as a gentleman planter, his daughters being in England and looking upon that country as their home.

The planters of the Georgia coast and islands were "men of parts" who had helped in the building of Georgia. John Couper had known it in pre-Revolutionary days, and the actors in that struggle were his familiar friends. His conversation, enriched by anecdote, was charming and instructing. Major Page had met and known the men who ruled the councils of the Provincial government. Poulain du Bignon had lived a life of varied experience. In India he had witnessed the Mogul Empire, with its barbaric splendor, crumble before British arms. Aid and chief of artillery to Hyder Ali, he had ridden victoriously over the rich plains of the Carnatic and led, in desperate charge, the wild Mahratta horsemen against the unyielding British square. In later years in

the brig *Josephine,* with letters of marque, stamped
with the lilies of France, he had sailed the waters
of the Caribbean, and skirted the Spanish Main.
At Bordeaux he had met the widowed Dame Osier,
married her, and drifted to the Georgia coast.
In 1793, he bought land on Jekyl Island, and now
was ending a wild and exciting life in a quiet island
home.

These men had seen life in many phases, and their
talk was not always of crops and the need of rain.
At times battles and sieges were recalled, and stories recounted of the great events of history.

The life on St. Simon's was a *mélange* of Old
World courtesy and refinement, intermixed with
a democratic simplicity. Only in the household
of Major Butler was there evidence of great wealth.
But everywhere were immense comfort and unbounded hospitality. To be a guest of one family
was to be a welcome visitor to all. The tables were
spread with home-grown viands, the glasses filled
with foreign wine and brandy. Whiskey was unknown. Rum punch always closed the evening.
The men were hard drinkers, but carried their
liquor well and were seldom overcome. If this
did occur, no disgrace followed, save the confes-
sion of a personal weakness.

Although Major Butler left the island in 1815,

he purchased the St. Clair house in 1820 and gave
it, for a nominal rent, to a club formed by the
planters of St. Simon's solely for social pleasure.
This was called the St. Clair Club, and here monthly
dinners were given, each member furnishing, in
rotation, dinner, service, wines, and punch. Great
emulation existed as to style and quality on these
occasions. Three outside guests were allowed to
be invited, and these came from St. Mary's southward to Savannah and as far as Augusta at the
north. The manners of the time warranting it,
the occasions were scenes of extraordinary convivi-
ality. The most surprising experiences and ad-
ventures were recounted, intermixed with song and
story, for the penalty was heavy for the one who
sang no song, told no story, and so declared himself
but a "niddling."

Charles Wylly pictures the dinner of December
7, 1821. The hour is 5 P.M. The slanting rays of
the sun crimson the green lawn and light the fes-
toons of moss draping the old oaks that shade the
house. Most magnificent of these is "Old England," with which no other could compare for size
of girth and spread of limb.

Inside, the dining room is made cheerful by the
glow of a great wood fire. The table, with places
for fourteen, is covered with the snowiest of

damasks, and lit by a score of candles, made from the wax of the myrtle berry that covers the salt marshes and placed in brass candlesticks that are polished like gold. The dishes are of blue East India china.

The host on this occasion is evidently Mr. John Couper, for the cook is the immortal Sans Foix and the waiters are Sandy, Johnny, and old Dick from Cannon's Point, assisted by James Dennison from the Village. Since nine in the morning they have been busy in the kitchen, and now, at five, all is in readiness.

The guests arriving — no one, whatever his age, so effeminate as to use carriage or chaise — are mounted on wiry steeds, whose living has been drawn from marsh moss and shucks, but who show in gait and mettle their descent from Spanish and Arab stock. Each one is accompanied by one or two black boys, eager for the fragments of the feast.

The club members present on this occasion were John Couper, John Fraser, Dr. William Fraser, Alexander Wylly, his son, Alexander William Wylly, William Page, Raymond Demere, George Baillie, Benjamin Cater, William Armstrong, and Daniel Heyward Brailsford. The three outside guests of the club were Captain Du Bignon of

Jekyl Island, Dr. James Troup of Darien, and Mr. Thomas Charlton of Savannah.

Dinners at that time on the coast were not served in courses, excepting the soup and dessert, everything else being placed on the table at once, and usually kept hot under highly polished covers of Britannia ware. Mr. James Hamilton had his covers made of silver, and left them by will to his daughter, Isabella Corbin de Dampière.

The guests seated themselves around the attractive table, and the dinner was served. Two soups, one a clam broth, the other a chicken mulligatawny, were brought on first. Then fish, shrimp pies, crab in shell, roasts, and vegetables were placed in one service. The dessert was simple — tartlets of orange marmalade, dried fruits, and nuts. The dishes disposed of, amid general gossip and talk, and the cloth removed, the great punch bowl was brought in, with its mixture of rum, brandy, sugar, lemon juice, and peel. The wine glasses were pushed aside, and stubby bottle-shaped glass mugs handed round. The chairman of the meeting, rising, announced that the health of the President of the United States would be drunk, standing and with cheers. Mr. Charlton, responding, said the thanks of the whole country were due President Monroe for his wise conduct of affairs.

After this opening of the evening there is much filling of mugs, nodding of heads one to another, with words of good wishes — "Happy days to you," and the like. Songs are called for, and Captain Du Bignon in a husky voice gives, "Cheer up, my lads. Cheer up!" Captain John Fraser follows in a fine tenor, with "A Valiant Soldier I Dare to Name," which is received with much applause. Dr. William Fraser is called upon for his Hindu song, a translation of which is: —

> Songster sweet, begin thy lay,
> Always fresh and ever gay.
> Bring me quick inspiring wine,
> Always fresh and ever fine,

to which Fiddler Johnny adds an accompaniment, with admiration on his glowing face.

The whole purpose of these dinners is not the mere enjoyment of eating and drinking, for there is much interesting conversation. George Baillie, who talks with knowledge and spirit on almost every subject, has been discussing Sheridan and Molière with his uncle, Captain Wylly, who observes, "Wit is only what everyone would have said, could he have thought of it." "Yes, dear Uncle," answers George. "Call in a good surgeon, and even yourself might be delivered of it."

Dr. Troup has been recounting to Major Page the incidents of his visit to an Indian cousin in the Alabama Creek Territory. He had visited that remarkable man, Alexander McGillivray, the virtual emperor of the Creeks, at Broken Arrow in the Coosa Valley. He tells of the beauty and fertility of the lands on the banks of the Coosa and Tallapoosa, and of the Indian villages, with their comfortable log cabins, gardens, and fields.

Dr. Fraser has been telling old Raymond Demere of the Mogul Empire, where diamonds, rubies, and pearls are the loot of the common soldier, and the eyes of the miserly man sparkle with covetousness.

Two hours pass in this pleasant way, when the chairman rises, raps smartly on the table for silence, and says, "Gentlemen, I propose the joint health of our esteemed friends, Mr. and Mrs. John Couper, and that of the boy presented by Mrs. Couper for the admiration of its father and every resident on the island — William Audley Couper. Waiter, fill every glass."

The toast is drunk enthusiastically.

Mr. Couper lifts his massive frame and stands erect. Then, clearing his throat, he says, "I thank you, my friends, for this honor. I should respond with song, but the condition of my throat forbids," and he then continues with an amusing anecdote that sets the table roaring, while his fiddler Johnny works frantically on his bow. Punch is ordered served all around, servants included, these imbibing their drinks in corners and hallways, wishing that club dinners were everyday occurrences.

Nine strikes, and "Auld Lang Syne" is sung standing with joined hands. The horses are called for, and Captain Wylly and Major Page are the first to say good-night. Attended by their faithful body servants, James Dennison and old Neptune, they ride away to the southward. The others follow, each with a black man, friend and servant, to ride behind if necessary, and help the brave souls back to the forgiveness of home. But in truth aid was not often needed, for "there were giants in those days."

The butlers of the old families were unique personalities. They were known as "Mr. Couper's man," "Mr. Wylly's man," and so on. Benbow of the Caters, Gibb of the Spaldings, Jack of the Troups, and especially Dick, who belonged to Major McIntosh, were perfect types of a vanished past. "Dick was the best-mannered man, white or black, I have ever known," writes Charles Wylly. "Once I accompanied my father, who called on Major McIntosh at Fair Hope. Dick came to the door and told us that his master and mistress were away from home, and would be grieved to have missed seeing Mr. Wylly. At that time not to have asked a guest to the sideboard for refreshment would have been a slur on the house, so, after a minute's pause, Dick added, 'Will not Mr. Wylly walk into the dining room?' We did, and Dick disappeared into the pantry. Returning with a black bottle, he said, with a bow, 'Master carried the keys with him, and Mr. Wylly will, I hope, excuse the absence of a decanter. Use this bottle, which I have pilfered from my Master, and, believe me, as I chose it, it is the best he has.'

"It was the noblest sacrifice to the honor of the Fair Hope plantation. A slave gave away his good name rather than have the home of a McIntosh suffer shame. In those days brandy was, in the South, a token as sacred as the bread and salt in Eastern lands. In the end Dick and his master died on the same day, on a steamboat between Columbus and Apalachicola, both seeming to have reached the same decision that life had been long enough."

The families who lived on St. Simon's were deeply attached to their island home, which was a truly beautiful one—surrounded by a world of marsh and bordered by a world of sea, the woodland drives overarched by majestic oaks fringed with long gray moss, the views of ocean and distant islands entrancing. The very air had a softness not felt elsewhere, and filled with the fragrance of flowers.

"But it is the historic associations interwoven with St. Simon's that give it its charm," wrote Canon Leigh of England. "Its soil is humanized and made dear by the spirits of those who have lived on and in its neighborhood."

Its marshes have been called "candid and simple and nothing-withholding and free," by Sidney Lanier, and few have breathed its sweet and clean salt air but have borne witness to its spell. Aaron Burr wrote of it, Basil Hall confessed it, Bartram lingered on its shore. Charles Lyell studied it, Miss Murray and Fredrika Bremer spoke of its attraction, and Fanny Kemble illustrated in burning words the beauty of its woods and the profusion and sweetness of its flowering shrubs and vines. To the islanders themselves it was the Eden of Georgia.

But there is a serpent in every Eden. St. Simon's lay in the path of tropical storms. The day before the hurricane of 1824, the weather was wild and threatening. Great masses of black clouds hurried before the ever-increasing wind, fringed with gleams of lightning. Heralded by rolls of thunder, they moved like a grand army in endless procession from north to south, their ally, the ocean, declaring an eternal war against the solid earth and the handwork of man. At twelve next day there was a sudden increase of violence, and at four trees were leveled in all directions, while the boom of the sea was one continuous roar. The sky was darkened by great flocks of gulls and curlews which, with shrill screams, sought shelter on the mainland.

At Mulberry Grove, the Demere home, there was an unvoiced terror, for the younger son had left for Darien that morning, maddened by an interview with his father, and the girl he loved had made him promise to return, and not spend the night on a debauch. Old Raymond Demere had wasted his youth in Charleston, and was now spending a crabbed old age on the island. A few years before he had brought back from Charleston a lovely young girl, named Mary, whom he called his ward. The inevitable happened, and the son and she fell in love. What took place on the morning of the hurricane no outsider ever knew, but the young man left for Darien in desperation.

That night, in fulfillment of his promise, he attempted to return across the sound in an open boat in the face of the hurricane, and was drowned.

From the Demere burial ground, dark under overhanging trees, the horizontal tombstones hardly visible in the undergrowth, a path leads through the deep woods to the sound. It is said that no footstep has disturbed the fallen leaves since Mary, the hapless girl of many sorrows, went down that path and drowned herself. It is a Haunted Way, a Ghost Walk, which is shunned to this day by the Negroes, who call it "Mary-de-Wander," and who will tell you that *Mary still walks that road.*

Another spot that they avoid is Eboe's Landing, between Gascoigne's Bluff and Frederica. The slave ships were said to have landed their cargoes here, and there is a tradition that a slave who had been a chief in his native land led a band of slaves through the woods to death in the sound, in preference to slavery.

But in spite of storms and tragedy, life on St. Simon's continued in the same simple, pleasant, and hospitable way. The social centre of the island was the little church, a rustic building under great broad-spreading oaks, about half a mile to the east of old Frederica on the road leading down to the Point. Christ Church, one of the oldest in Georgia, was well supported and well attended. On Sundays one service was held at 11 A.M. for the whites, and in the afternoon a lecture was given for the colored people.

This church had the distinction of being the only one in Georgia to which, on each Easter Monday, a clerk and pew opener were elected. The clerk — pronounced "clark" by the congregation — was for many years the venerable Mr. Davis. He sat on a high seat immediately in front of the officiating priest, and led the responses in a fine bass voice. The pew opener was a remarkable and interesting character. During her long residence on the island this lady told no one of the accident by which she had lost her "limb." She had a great liking for young Alexander Wylly, Captain Wylly's oldest son, and when, consumed by curiosity, he had the temerity to ask her, she said, "I will tell you, Alexander, if you promise not to ask another question about it." He promised, and she said, "'T was bit off," leaving him as much in the dark as before.

On Sunday morning at nine o'clock the congregation commenced to arrive by gig and chaise, the older ladies wearing calashes made of wired green silk, a sort of miniature buggy top, which was laid aside upon entering the pew. They then gathered for gossip, which did not cease until the "Dearly Beloved" was uttered by the preacher. The men, on arriving, seated themselves outside on benches under the trees, received their mail, which was brought to the church by the postmaster, read letters, and discussed the latest news from Milledgeville, Charleston, and Washington. The children played in the shade until all were summoned in to worship.

At one time there was a dissension in the church. A dispute known as "Organ or no organ" raged. Mr. John Couper had taught his man Johnson to play on the pipes, and when requested to decide the question he sent Johnny to the next Sunday's service with his bagpipe and a note, in which he recommended the churchwardens to "try the pipes as a compromise."

Dr. Grant, who lived at Oatlands, was the head warden of the church, as well as the physician of the island. He was a native of New Jersey and the very antithesis of his neighbors; a shrewd business man, a lender, not a borrower, of money, who became in time very rich. He was an estimable man, though George Baillie said of him, "He is such a bore with his many excellencies as to make me detest every Christian virtue."

Dr. Grant probably disapproved quite as highly

of the *bon vivants* of the St. Clair Club, as we do not hear of his attending their hilarious meetings, at which, by the end of the evening, all the members were equally ready for tears or laughter.

Nor was he, probably, a member of the Agricultural and Sporting Club, of which Captain Fraser was President, Colonel Hazzard Vice President, and Mr. James Gould Secretary and Treasurer.

This club exchanged civilities with the Camden Hunt Club on the mainland, of which General Charles Floyd was President. Organized in 1827, it had fifteen regular and nineteen honorary members, Mr. Nightengale being one of the former. Among the latter were Thomas Bryan of Broughton Island, Henry Du Bignon of Jekyl, and John Fraser, W. W. Hazzard, James Gould, and Thomas Butler King of St. Simon's. Appended to the list of members of this date is an interesting footnote by the Secretary: —

J. Morrison — Stricken off the list as a matter of course. Cowards and liars not being considered as eligible to membership.

The Camden Club members met and hunted twice a month, the game consisting of "deer, bear, pigs, cows, bulls, wild cats, and turkeys."

Minutes were kept of these meetings, one of them being as follows: —

CLUB MEETING NO. 16.
AT SHELBINE. *On Saturday, Jan. 30th* 1836.

Benjamin Hopkins, T. E. Hardee, John Dilworth and Robert Floyd met at Jones' Road at 9 o'clock and hunted. Gen. John Floyd and Sam Floyd were at dinner.

The Hunt:

Put the hounds in the tall swamp. After a short trail, "full cry" was heard, and very soon two deer were brought out to Benjamin Hopkins, who slew one on the spot, a doe, 30 yards. He fired both barrels. Ben Hopkins and T. Hardee then retired from the field, and Dilworth and R. Floyd continued the hunt. Drove Couper's swamp. D. fired at three deer with rifle, 100 yards. The dogs ran them into Brownlee's Swamp, and in about 20 minutes brought out one, a buck, to D. and he fired at him 70 yards and wounded him badly. We saw much blood, but the deer escaped. On an open burn three deer got up and ran off, and R. Floyd and Dilworth fired at them, 40 yards, 3 shots, and wounded two very badly, then gave chase, and after separating the one most hurt, ran it rapidly for ¼ of a mile, then captured it. The woods were so open, that the deer was in sight all the time, and no dogs were present to assist. They then retired to Shelbine, and dined.

One of the rules of the Camden Hunt Club was that no member should be left alone in the woods, unless he desired to be.

Whether the Sporting Club of St. Simon's followed the plan of the Camden Club is not known. Its members would probably have had to hunt deer on the mainland, as by this time the island was entirely settled and there was no great extent of woodland left.

Of one courtesy paid the Camden Club we know, as in January 1836 the following invitation was sent to its members: —

CLUB HOUSE, ST. SIMON'S.

The Agricultural and Sporting Club of St. Simon's request the honour of the company of the Camden Club, and the members' ladies, at Frederica on the 6th of February next, the Centennial Anniversary of the landing of General Oglethorpe.

(Signed) JAMES F. GOULD.
Sec. & Treasurer of the A. & S. Club.

Frederica, which was known as "Old Town," was at this time not much more than a heap of ruins, but there is no doubt that the visitors, who rowed up in their boats from Camden County, received a hospitable welcome from the inhabitants of St.

Simon's, and spent a delightful day. An abundant feast was probably spread on that same "carpet of grass beneath the live-oaks" where the ladies of Oglethorpe's day had "flaunted their gowns."

As speeches were the fashion of the day, many were probably delivered, the most edifying by Mr. Thomas Spalding of Sapelo, who had written a Life of General Oglethorpe for the Georgia Historical Society.

Having the same interests, and the same problems to solve, these men of the Georgia coast must have thoroughly enjoyed such reunions, where they could tell of their experiences and exchange ideas.

If great generosity of heart, great honesty of purpose, and unblemished integrity can outweigh the faults arising from impulse and excesses in a great measure attributable to the habits of the day, then these men of the Old South have little to fear in the judgment yet to be meted out.

VIII

THE SECOND GENERATION

WITH the first quarter of the nineteenth century a younger generation had grown up on St. Simon's Island.

Mr. and Mrs. John Couper had five children — James Hamilton, Ann, John, Isabel, and William Audley. The only one of outstanding ability was the oldest son, who had been named after Mr. James Hamilton, Mr. Couper's friend and partner.

At the age of eight little James was sent to school in New Haven, accompanied by his "black boy," Sandy.

In his first letter, he writes, "Dear Pappa, I have the opportunity of writing you a few lines. I am well and hope you are well also, and my mother and brother and sister   my boy Sandy is well   I like the place very well but I don't like it so well as St. Simon's." Two months later, "You asked me what hours I have to go to school   I have to go to school at nine in the morning and stay until twelve

and in the afternoon I go at two and stay until five."
Six hours of study for a little boy of eight!

In the winter of 1804 he wrote, "It snowed the
other day   We had fine fun heaving the snow balls
at each other." It was not much fun for the "black
boy" however, for his little master wrote in March,
"Sandy was very sick   They thought he would
dy   But he is now well." To this piece of news,
he adds, "I would be very glad if you would send
me a little Money to buy Books with   I find Money
a very useful thing heare   I cant get anything here
without Money." In a postscript he is reproach-
ful. "I have writ you before for some Money
but have not received no answer   I received forty
Dollars a good while ago." Two months later,
he writes, "I have received fifty Dollars from
Mama, which I thank you and Mama very much
for it." And he ends, "Give my respects to Mr.
Craig   Tell him he is not so good as his word
Tell him that he told me he would write me   Tell
him that I remain as good as my word." Which
he did, to the end of his life.

At fourteen, James Hamilton was sent to St.
Mary's College in Maryland, and eventually he
went to Yale, where he graduated in 1814, sharing
honors with his roommate and best friend, John
Lord of New York. Coming home, he began to

work for his father, and in 1816, at the age of twenty-three, was given entire charge of Hopeton, the Couper-Hamilton plantation on the Altamaha.

At the Village, below Cannon's Point, another large family of young people was growing up. The Alexander Wyllys had two sons, Alexander William and John, and six daughters, all of whom reached maturity.

Benjamin Cater, the little boy whose life had been saved by the old family servant, Benbow, had been well educated by his guardian, Major Page, and on graduating at Yale had returned to St. Simon's and come into his property, Kelvyn Grove.

At Retreat, the only child, little Anne Page, had received a most careful training by a devoted father and mother, who were determined that she should not be spoiled. They wisely decided that she must not be educated alone, but should join the classes of other children and have their companionship.

General John Floyd, who lived in Camden County, opposite Cumberland Island, had a teacher for his tall sons and daughters, and to his place the little girl was sent on Monday mornings, in the eight-oared rowboat which had been named in her honor, "The Anne." In the same way she returned to Retreat every Saturday. Later on she was taught French by the lovely Mrs. Henry Du Bignon, with the latter's own children. And finally she joined the class of her friends at Cannon's Point, where Mr. Brown, who had been educated at Oxford, taught in Mr. John Couper's family for two generations.

A pretty picture is given of Retreat by Mrs. Hamilton Couper, who was at this time little Caroline Wylly of St. Clair: —

Before day-light Mama would come up and tap on our little hands and say, "Come — get up — get up — we are going down to Retreat." So up we would get, and Marote would dress us, and down stairs we would go, and Mama and Papa were ready, and there were the two double gigs. Papa drove Mama and two of us in one, with the big bay horse called Andrew Jackson. Sister Fannie and two others went in the other gig with Bouncer, the big white horse, and Nero, the groom, rode by on horseback. It was always understood that the Armstrongs would go at the same time, and as The Village was below St. Clair, the signal, if they had passed the cross road first, would be a bunch of green left in the middle of the road. We generally got to Observation Pond just as the sun was rising, and then how beautiful Retreat was as we came into the yard! So clean, and everything in order, with such comfort everywhere. Always we found Mrs. Page standing in the front door,

dressed in the most spotless white, with a cap like
snow on her head, and three blue gauze bows in
front. She was so fair and sweet. Such a fine
woman and beloved by everybody.

Major Page was so intelligent. He and Papa
would talk business, and Mama and Mrs. Page
would talk about everything! Then came Lady
to say breakfast was ready. Such a nice breakfast! Mrs. Page was famous for her beautiful
cooking and housekeeping. Such broiled chicken!
Such breads! I never saw such waffles. Then
the dinner. *So* nice. Such ducks and ham and
every delicacy. Such desserts! Mrs. Page made
puddings as no one else could, of arrowroot, and a
delicious sauce as light as a feather.

After breakfast Mama was asked to step to the
end of the piazza, and there outside were all the
family servants to speak to her. There was Joan,
the cook, Old Betty, Polly and Lilla, Rutty and the
others, Lady standing by herself, as she considered
herself the head.

Abby our head-nurse, had recommended a little
boy named Sam, to sweep the yard and brush the
flies, and he proved to be such a good and trusty
little boy. His father's name was Jim-Gwine-
Run-Away. During the war of 1812, he tried
to go to the British, but the Old Estate Negroes
stopped him, and afterwards always called him Jim-
Gwine-Run-Away. Sam grew up to be the trusted
factotum of the King family.

Retreat was a dear old place with the beautiful

trees and flowers, and the view of the Atlantic
and the Sound, with Jekyl, and two or three vessels
at anchor.

In 1816, just before the end of the War of 1812,
Major Page moved with his family and a number
of slaves to Darien, to avoid the British, who were
threatening the coast. He was persuaded to allow Anne to join Mrs. John Couper's party, and
spend Christmas at Dungeness on Cumberland
Island.

Dungeness, that great old four-storied tabby
house, had thirty rooms. A terrace led down from
the rear into a garden, where dates, bananas, and
olives grew. In front of the house was a grove of
live oaks, from which a road led down to the beach,
with its fine surf bathing.

At this delightful home Mrs. Couper and her gay
party of young people were having a pleasant time,
when the British, under Admiral Cockburn, took
possession of the island, and made Dungeness
their headquarters. James Hamilton Couper, as
the man of the party, forbade his sister Ann and
her friends to come downstairs. The Admiral
asked for them, however, and, highly pleased to
dine with the great man on his service of silver
plate, the girls dressed in their best, and trooped

down in spite of the disapproval of young Mr. Couper. Anne Page was the youngest of the party, and, burning her lips on the hot silver coffee cup, she uttered an exclamation. The older girls were shocked at her simplicity, but she had the best of them when James Couper told the Admiral that the property on the south end of St. Simon's belonged to "this little girl" and the Admiral promised to protect it.

He kept his word, for although the British were on St. Simon's for three weeks, Retreat was never disturbed.

The last battle of the War of 1812 was fought on Cumberland Island, when the British were driven away by Captain Messias.

Anne Page grew up to be a lovely and accomplished woman. She inherited from her father a beautiful voice, and kept up her music to the end of her life. Gentle and considerate, she won everyone by her pleasing manners, and was admired by old as well as young. In her album, such as every girl kept at that time, Captain Wylly wrote these lines: —

"Good sense, good nature and good breeding
    Went upon a pilgrimage.
    They visited the fair of every clime,
    And rested with Anne Page."

THE SECOND GENERATION   145

There were several families on St. Simon's with daughters about the age of Anne Page, — the Coupers, Wyllys, Grants, and Armstrongs. When Anne would receive a box of pretty frocks from England, she would send them up the island, to share the fashions with her friends, and the frocks usually returned the worse for many tryings on.

Growing up as an only child, Anne Page was considered an heiress, and when she became a young lady had many suitors, among them several brothers of her friends.   A little fat man named Jenner, seeking an heiress to mend his fortunes, was equally attentive to Miss Page and Miss Grant.   When he dropped on his knees and proposed to Anne, she said, "I thought your attentions were to Miss Grant."   Clapping his hands to his bald head, and weeping, the fat little man said, "Miss Grant is not Miss Page."   The identical scene occurred the next day at the home of Miss Grant, to the great amusement of the two girls.

By this time Anne had developed a real business talent, and in the summer of 1823, while her father was at Saratoga, she took entire charge of the place, looking carefully into every detail and sending her father and his factors in Savannah an account of all that was being done.

In 1824, Anne Page married the Honorable

Thomas Butler King, the son of Captain Daniel King and of Hannah Lord, of Hartford, Connecticut. Mr. King had sudied law, but before graduating had been obliged to come South with an invalid brother, and, meeting Miss Page, had fallen in love with her.

Thomas Butler King was himself sound in health of body and mind, and a man of temperate habits and untiring energy. He had a cheerful disposition, great kindness of heart, and much personal charm. He increased the plantation left by Mr. Page, and introduced improvements in drainage and cultivation far in advance of his time. He devoted himself to the well-being of his Negroes and was repaid by a touching love, their slaves often saying, "No gentleman like our Massa!" His daughter Florence wrote years later, "On his return home, how often have I seen them crowd around him, kissing his hands, he with a kindly word for each one."

Mr. King entered public life in 1832, representing Georgia in Congress, where he stayed for sixteen years. As Chairman of Naval Affairs, he established the Pacific Mail and instigated other beneficial legislation.

By 1825, James Hamilton Couper had managed the Hopeton property so successfully that it was

JAMES HAMILTON COUPER   CAROLINE WYLLY COUPER

acknowledged to be a model plantation. In that year he went to Europe to study the diking system of Holland, with a view to improving the ditching of his rice fields. On the way he went to Scotland to visit his father's family in Glasgow, and so pleased were they with their American. nephew that his Uncle James, who was Professor of Astronomy at the University, wrote to his father, "I am disposed to think you may live to see him one of the most eminent characters in his age and country."

In 1827, James Hamilton Couper married Caroline Georgia Wylly, the youngest child of Captain and Mrs. Wylly. He was at this time thirty-three and she was sixteen.

A letter from old John Couper, written to his brother James the following year, gives his own situation.

St. Simon's.   *24th May* 1828.

My dear Brother,

It is long since I wrote you and longer since I heard from you. I hope to hear oftener, and promise better behaviour. Since I wrote you last (As we Yankys say) I guess a considerable change has taken place in my concerns. Something like a bankruptcy. I have however paid all my debts *in full,* and have a competence left.

You know I commenced planting without capital, of course had to go in debt, and 8% compound interest I find to be the real perpetual motion. Though tolerable successful I had sad reverses. Embargoes, non-intercourse, and war interfered with my prospects, whilst *interest* progressed. My loss of 80 prime and effective Negroes — carried off by the enemy — lessened my annual income full $15,000. To supply their place *in part,* I bought 120 slaves, for which I paid an average of $450. Crops were not favorable in 1824. I had matured a crop of 800 bales of cotton which would have produced $90,000. This was lost in 12 hours by hurricane. In 1825 I again nearly lost my crop by caterpillars. Cotton then sunk in price without any prospect of improvement. Lands were reduced to one half their value, and slaves to $250 or $200. In short I saw no hope of paying off my debts and retaining my property, and though not pushed I thought it best during my life to meet the storm. So — to make a long story short — Mr. Hamilton being my principal creditor — on he agreeing to pay what other debts I owed, I surrendered to him all my property, debts and dues of every description, in a lump without valuation, except my lands on St. Simon's and a hundred slaves.

So on the first day of January 1827, I was thrown on the world without a dollar to support my people and family — and glad to get off so well. Though at a reasonable valuation the property surrendered

was more than sufficient to pay my debts, yet had
it been brought to a forced sale, it might have done
less.   I am satisfied and relieved of much anxiety.
By this event neither my standing in society, nor
my mode of living have suffered any change.

Mr. Hamilton has sold one half of the plantation,
Hopeton, to my son James, at the rate of $80,000.
Had I been able to retain it, I should not have taken
$150,000.   Also the half of 300 slaves, which I
gave at $300, retaining the other half himself.
James has sixteen years credit, interest at 6%.   He
has the entire management, for which he receives
$3,000 per annum, with the run of the plantation.
He had $9,000 acquired by his industry.   He was
fortunate in making a good crop last year, both
corn and cotton, and has a favorable prospect this
year.

He is now engaged erecting sugar works — ex-
pects a steam engine from Bolton and Wats of Birmingham, and a sugar mill and boilers from Liverpool.   All these articles could be got much cheaper
in this country, but we believe English engines
(particularly from Bolton and Wats) are more to
be depended on, and any failure, where repairs are
not easily obtained, might endanger the loss of a
crop.   James has confined himself this year to the
planting of as many cane as will furnish seed for
about 250 acres in 1829.   He afterwards means to
increase to 400.   Annually to alternate with rice,
besides planting a portion of cotton.

In addition to this undertaking he has taken unto himself a wife. A very good girl, only 17 years old. We were all pleased with the match.

My son John has been now two years settled for himself in the wild woods of America (Florida) among the bears and tigers, upon a piece of good land in the centre of a large swamp. I should describe the situation, though I have never been there, but Mr. Fraser will give you a better account, as he is settling a place adjoining. The first year John depended upon the gun for subsistence. He now boasts of being a good liver, having cattle, sheep and poultry about him. Mr. Fraser will tell you of the approach to John's *den* by torchlight. Equal in grandeur to the approach of Telemaclar to the I R.

Mrs. Fraser and family are still with us. She now has five children, one boy and four girls, all fine healthy children. My daughter Isabella is near 13 years — *quite a blue stocking* — but too much of the Couper in appearance to be handsome. I beg my fair cousins' pardon. I don't include them. My son William, now near 11, is an idle boy, and would sooner walk a mile to race home on a plough horse than learn his lessons. I however intend to make a philosopher of him. Next year shall send him to an academy at Northampton, Massachusetts, and when he has laid in a sufficient amount of Yankee cunning, I shall send him to Berlin, in order to un-learn roguery, and gain honour — German principles. At about 24 he may return home, to plant cowpeas and pumpkins, and eat fat meat, as his father has done.

Mrs. Couper enjoys good health and is rather en bon point.   As to myself I feel the effects of old age fast approaching, but am still able to look after my business.   As we have no stepping stone here, I find I have to lead my horse to a log to get my foot in the stirrup.   Whether this is from old age or corpulence I know not, but I believe a little of both.

Mr. Fraser has to visit England about his commission, which I hope he may lose.   He promises to call on you, and to him I refer you for every information respecting the tribe of Coupers in Georgia.   We have had some talk of getting a governess for our female children.   I do not know whether there are any such articles in Scotland, but if Mr. F. requires your advice, I beg you to afford it.

I recently asked James Couper if he had wrote to you or any of his relations since his return.   He says he is ashamed that he has not, but said he would soon break the ice.   He left us a few days ago, with his *rib,* for his summer residence in Wayne County.

Mrs. Couper joins me in our best and kindest regards to you and Mrs. Couper, Miss Couper and your sons.   Please also remember me to my brother William, and Mrs. Lynn, and their families.

I am my dear brother most affectionately your's,

JOHN COUPER.

Mr. Couper was at this time sixty-nine, and was to live to be ninety.

Three years after Caroline Wylly married James Hamilton Couper, her oldest brother, Alexander William, made what might be called a runaway match with Elizabeth, one of the Spalding heiresses. His mother was notified by the following letter, written by her sister, Susan Armstrong, who was then living in Darien.

DARIEN, *March 12th*, 1830.

MY DEAR SISTER:

I promised our dear Alexander to write and inform you that he was married this morning to Miss Spalding, *at my house.* I was taken by surprise. He called this morning before I was out of bed, and desired James to say he requested me to rise, that he would be back in half an hour. In a short time after Miss Spalding and Miss Rice came; then followed Anne Wylly. And then came Dr. Bond, Mr. James Bond and Mr. Lafil, the magistrate who married them. But Elizabeth thought her mother would not be satisfied unless the ceremony was performed by a clergyman. As soon therefore as your son John and Matilda arrived from Hopeton, John went for Mr. Pratt, who married them again. About an hour ago they left this, accompanied by John and Matilda, and will remain at Hopeton a few days.

I was not in the secret, and in no way instrumental in withdrawing E. from her *duty,* but I think she was not wrong in seeking her own happiness and that of another, the one most dear to her. Had he been a worthless profligate, her parents would have been excusable. I have no doubt Mr. and Mrs. Spalding will be provoked with me, but what could I do, when taken by surprise, by *Love, Law and Physic, aided by Divinity?* For the interest and happiness of Alexander, I will always be ready to act as far as is in my poor power. I trust I shall never be called upon to do what is improper. They have my blessing and most ardent wish for their happiness. In a short time I hope the *fermentation* will subside and all be clear and calm. You will no doubt hear from Anne. I am bewildered which must plead my excuse for a hasty scrawl. Give my love to Captain Wylly and to Harriet, and believe me, your affectionate sister

S. ARMSTRONG.

This Susan Armstrong must have come with the other Armstrong relatives from Nassau when Captain Wylly and his family moved to St. Simon's. She evidently had a weakness for her nephew, William Alexander, and must have been pleased when the young couple were forgiven and came to live in the neighborhood of Darien at the Forest on Sapelo River. This place, which had belonged to William McIntosh, the great-grandfather of

Elizabeth Spalding, was noted for the spaciousness and beauty of its lawn, where pains had been taken to plant every indigenous tree.

Darien, at this time one of the two largest cotton ports in the state, was a pleasant place to live in. Several of the houses must have been handsome — Dr. Troup's for instance, which was designed by the English architect Jay, who built the famous Habersham and Owens houses in Savannah. Few of its inhabitants stayed there in summer, but migrated to the Ridge, three miles away, a charming settlement on a bluff overlooking the salt marshes. Here, on either side of a wide shell road, were delightful summer homes, surrounded by broad piazzas, within reach of the cool sea breezes and beyond the reach of the deadly "miasma" which, at that time, was thought to cause the fatal fevers of the low lands.

In the *Darien Gazette* of October 20, 1836, appeared the following notice: —

A son, we learn, was born on the 16th instant to our friends, Mr. and Mrs. Alexander William Wylly. The event occurred at The Thicket, the home of Captain Charles Spalding, U. S. A, 2nd Dragoons, who is serving with his regiment in Florida. We offer our congratulations.

This third son of the family was named Charles Spalding Wylly, after the uncle at whose house he was born. Gifted with rare powers of mind and heart, keenly interested in human nature, responsive and sympathetic, he was destined to become a most interesting and original character, and, strong as the primal man, to outlive every member but one of his large family, and to see the complete passing away of the old coast civilization.

IX

THE WRECK OF THE "PULASKI"

THE ten years that followed the marriage of James
Hamilton Couper were spent happily with his wife
and children at Hopeton, which had, by this time,
become the best-managed plantation in Georgia.

In the summer of 1838, having business to attend
to in New York, Mr. Couper embarked on the
steamship *Pulaski*, which left Savannah on June
14. He had in his charge his sister-in-law, Mrs.
William Fraser, with her little son Menzies, and
Mrs. Nightengale of Dungeness with her baby
girl Louisa. The vessel was filled with many
prominent people from Savannah and Charleston,
who had been attracted by the notice of the voyage
posted in Charleston: "One Night at Sea."

The first letter received from James Hamilton
Couper after the sailing of the *Pulaski* was headed,
"10 miles South of New River Inlet, North Carolina, 16th June, 1838," and began with these words,
"We are all safe after a most miraculous escape
from the awful destruction of the *Pulaski*."

His description of that event follows: —

The steam-ship *Pulaski,* Captain Dubois, left Savannah at 8 oclock on Wednesday morning, the 13th of June, with about 80 passengers. and a crew of 37.   She arrived at Charleston the same afternoon, and departed at 6 oclock the next morning for Baltimore, with about 65 additional passengers.

Of the passengers about 45 were females, and from 15 to 20 were children.   It was the period of the year when the usual summer migration from the South to the North was at its height, and as the *Pulaski* was a favorite boat, particularly in Savannah, the passengers consisted of some of the most respectable persons of Georgia and South Carolina, embracing in several instances, every, and in many, most of the members of distinguished families. Attracted by the reputation of the packet, the shortness of the voyage, and the circumstance that it would embrace only one night at sea, many persons had come to Savannah from distant points, to embark on the *Pulaski.*   Among whom may be particularly mentioned Judge Rochester of New York and a party of 11 from Florida.   From Savannah were Mr. G. E. Lamar, wife and 7 children, being every member of his immediate family.   Mr. Parkman with three daughters and a son; Mr.

Hutchinson, wife and two children; Dr. Cumming and lady; Mrs. William Mackay and two children, with many others.

The *Pulaski,* dressed out gaily in her flags, crossed the bar of Charleston between 7 and 8 o'clock. The weather was clear and apparently settled, the wind blowing freshly from the south east, and both sky and sea giving every promise of a safe and pleasant voyage. The appearance and feelings of the passengers were in harmony with the elements; cheerfulness and pleasure depicted in every countenance; and the observation was general that to travel in such a way was truly a mere jaunt of pleasure.

As the day advanced the wind increased in force, and shifted to the East: during the latter part of the afternoon the waves became high, and the vessel rolled so much that most of the ladies retired to their berths, and at tea many of the gentlemen were missing. About sun-set the clouds began to muster heavily towards the North East, and predictions were made that a gale was brewing in that quarter. At 9 however the clouds had very generally dispersed, and the stars shone out brilliantly above; beneath the sea heaved in long waves, the inky darkness of which was relieved only as the wind broke their crests into wreaths of snowy foam. The sea, striking the vessel under the

weather bow, and impeding her progress, a full
pressure of steam was given to enable her to overcome the resistance, which she did in gallant style;
and at 10 oclock, when I left the deck, she was dashing through the water at the rate of 11 miles an
hour, with a steadiness and ease, which indicated
power, but no unusual effort. At this time nearly
all the passengers had retired from the deck to the
cabins, where a few still continued to read or con-
verse until half after 10, when the last stragglers
went to their berths, anticipating a quiet and re-
freshing night's rest. Having exchanged with
Colonel and Mrs. Dunham, who occupied the next
berth to my own, and with whom I had been con-
versing, the usual wishes for a pleasant night's
rest, undressing myself, I fell into a sound slumber.

I could not have been asleep more than a half
hour, when I was suddenly waked by a deep, hol-
low and heavy sound, like the discharge of a battery of cannon at a short distance, which was instantly followed by a concussion of the air, a
universal tremor of the vessel, and a loud general
crash, as if the sides and deck had by some irresistible force been crushed together. The report and
the crash left no doubt that the boiler had exploded,
and as I sprang up from my berth, the conviction
was strong in my mind, that the vessel was in a
sinking condition.

The lights having been extinguished where I was in the after cabin by the concussion of the air, it was some moments before I could ascertain the position of the companion stairway, and it was only after stumbling over the floor, which was torn up, that, by placing my hands on the table, and following it along, I perceived the light at the head of the stairway. On reaching the deck I proceeded to the door of the ladies' cabin, which was above that of the gentlemen's, with the intention of seeing the two ladies who were under my charge, with the double object of calming their fears, and of placing them where I could find them. At the door I met ladies with their children, all in their night dresses, huddled together with an expression of wild dismay and horror depicted on every countenance, and anxiously inquiring what was the matter. I called for the ladies under my care, when Mrs. Fraser, holding her son by the hand, answered and came to me. I requested her to be composed, and not to leave that spot until I could ascertain the character of the accident, and return to her.

Proceeding over the fragments of glass, with which the deck was strewn, and which cut my feet, I met several persons crying out that the boat was on fire, and calling for buckets and water.

For an instant I turned, but, reflecting that the fire must soon be checked by the leaks, I proceeded over the starboard deck to the centre of the vessel where the engine was placed. The scene of wild destruction which there presented itself precluded all hope of safety, and rendered it certain that the vessel must sink in a very few minutes.

The promenade deck and wheel-house, which were above the boiler, with the staterooms on the right side, were all blown off, the decks ripped up, the bar-room and bulkhead between the boilers and forward cabin were crushed, and the right side of the hull so shattered, that the sea rushed in most fearfully. The boiler appeared to have been rent in the top throughout its whole length, and the end next to the bow of the boat burst out on the right side.

The left boiler and that side of the vessel were comparatively uninjured; in consequence of which she careened over to the left, and fortunately threw the shattered side partly out of water. As she however soon fell into the trough of the sea, at every roll the water rushed in, and increased in quantity as she settled down. Perceiving that the boat was inevitably and rapidly sinking, I returned towards the stern.

As I reached the companion-way of the after

cabin, I met a poor wretch dragging himself on the deck, and calling out most piteously, "O God, both of my legs are blown off!" He was the barber whose shop was near the boilers.

At this moment the ladies' cabin and the deck in front of it presented a heart-rending spectacle. Ladies, children and men, all in their night-clothes, were grouped together. The wildest confusion, alarm and despair marked the countenances of the ladies, while the gentlemen were anxiously seeking for their wives and children, and endeavoring to calm their fears by holding out hopes which they knew to be utterly vain. There were frantic calls for husbands and children, despairing inquiries if there were no hope of safety, horror and utter dismay; but there was little shrieking. The shock was as yet too sudden and stupefying, the danger too undefined for loud exclamations of grief or alarm. There seemed to be a general deep and appalling feeling that some overwhelming calamity had occurred, but as yet everything was uncertain and undefined.

As I reached the companion-way of the gentlemen's cabin, I stood still for a moment to rally myself. I felt the final hour of my existence had arrived, that there was no possible escape, and I summoned up all my energies to meet my fate with calmness and fortitude. The image of my wife, children, father and mother flashed before my mind; the bitter pang of the last separation wrung my soul for an instant; the struggle was over, and I was collected and ready to meet the emergency.

My thoughts were now directed to the ladies and children under my care, whose helpless and dependent situation called for every effort to save them. Immediately descending to my berth, I drew on my pantaloons, and made the mental inquiry what articles of clothing would be most useful. Boots and shoes were rejected as too cumbrous for swimming; and, throwing a large camlet cloak over my arm, for the protection of the ladies and children, I reached the deck, and passed rapidly to the starboard quarter, where I had noticed one of the small yawls hanging, and many settees and tables. As I got to it I found two of the crew casting off the ropes, in the act of lowering the boat. I had now but to spring in, and my individual safety was insured. The ladies were however not there. The time lost in searching for them would probably deprive me of this only chance of life, but the occasion called for the risk.

Proceeding to the door of the ladies' cabin, and assuming as calm a tone as I could, I called for the ladies under my care. They immediately replied. Merely observing, "Follow me, ladies," I turned toward the yawl and they followed. We had not proceeded far when Mrs. Fraser's foot slipped, and she fell with her son. I turned to assist her, but before I reached her she had recovered. This accident placed Mrs. Nightengale in advance, and by the time I got up with her, she had reached the boat. The hands were in it, and had nearly lowered it down to the water. Taking the infant from Mrs. Nightengale, I assisted her on to the bulwarks, and requested her to jump into the boat, which she immediately did, a distance of 10 feet. Her fall was fortunately broken by striking on one of the persons in the boat. Perceiving that the boat was about to be shoved off, I then sprang down with the infant in my arms. The yawl surged off as I sprang, my feet struck the gunwale, and I fell backwards into the sea. When I rose to the surface, I regained the boat, and threw the infant into its mother's arms. Getting in I requested Mrs. Fraser to throw down her son, which she immediately did. I caught him and called to her to jump herself. She fell into my arms, and the whole of our party were safe in the yawl. The next instant it was shoved off.

As I looked up the side of the steamship was

thronged with persons, calling out, "Hold on to that boat. Don't shove off that boat." In another instant, had not the boat been pushed away, they would have precipitated themselves in a mass upon us, and sunk it.

There are moments in life when the escape from impending danger has exceeded all possible hope, that the belief in an overruling Providence is felt with irresistible force. The heart then overflowing with gratitude, bows with deep-felt thankfulness to the hand that has been stretched out to save. Never were persons in a situation more calculated to inspire such a feeling than we were at this moment.

When the yawl left the side of the *Pulaski*, it was agreed that we should place ourselves at such a distance from her as to be beyond the vortex, if she sank suddenly, and yet near enough to regain her, if, contrary to our expectations, she continued to float. In pursuance of this intention, the yawl was allowed to drift about 150 yards astern of the steamer; and, keeping her head on to the sea, the two sailors, who had taken the oars, endeavored to preserve that distance.

Having accomplished the great object of getting out of the sinking vessel, our attention was now directed to our own situation. We found ourselves in a small yawl from 16 to 18 feet long, crowded with 12 persons, who consisted, besides the ladies and children under my care, of Captain Porter and son, Mr. William Robertson, a seaman (alias Barney), a Negro waiter (Solomon), and two Negro women. For some minutes it was doubtful whether the boat could live in the sea, or whether she could be kept from filling with water. She leaked badly, and the only article to bail her with was a slipper of one of the Negro women. The wind was blowing freshly, and the sea running high, and there were but two oars in the boat with which to manage her. These dangers however appeared small to that which had just been escaped, and there was a feeling of comparative safety. The two seamen, rowing to keep the head of the boat to the sea and to avoid drifting, and one person bailing incessantly, we remained at 100 to 200 yards from the Pulaski, waiting with feelings of intensely painful anxiety, the closing scene of the awful catastrophe. The wind was blowing keenly from the East, the sea rolling in heavy black waves below us, whilst the sky was partially obscured by flying clouds. The galley lights of the steamer were still burning brilliantly, and, as she rose and fell with the heaving ocean, she appeared as if illuminated for some fête. This brilliant and holi-

day appearance, compared with the utter wretched-
ness and despair of the helpless human beings in
her, who were rapidly approaching that awful moment when the ocean was to swallow them up, presented a contrast most touching and painful.

From our position we could perceive that she was
fast settling in the water, and, in profound silence,
and with the most intensely painful feelings, we
awaited the moment when nearly 200 human beings, many of them our intimate friends, were to
experience the agony of the last mortal struggle,
in the darkness of night, on the wild abyss of the
ocean, remote from human succor, and suddenly
called from the deep slumber which had followed a
day of happiness, to meet, not only a fearful death
themselves, but to witness the expiring agonies, and
to hear the dying shrieks of those most dear to
them.

The mass above the waters gradually diminished,
and, in a moment, every light was extinguished
and all was darkness. As the water rose to the
upper deck, a single wave had swept over the whole
of the galley lights; and with them hope seemed
also to be extinguished.

Soon afterwards a heavy crash was heard, followed by a loud and piercing shriek. The boat
had broken in two; then came the crackling of

planks, as if the decks were breaking up; shrill, wild and prolonged shrieks ensued, with the agonizing cry of the dying; all rising at once and ringing wildly over the waste of waters. In a few moments the burst of despair and agony had ceased; most of the sufferers had experienced the short and bitter pang of death, and had sunk to rise no more. And now were heard the long and deep hallos for assistance from persons who were clinging to such fragments of the wreck as they had grasped when they were precipitated into the ocean.

Soon after this the other quarter-boat, under the charge of the mate, Mr. Hibbert, came near us. Having hailed each other, it was agreed that we should keep together to render such mutual assistance as might be in our power. Understanding that we were in a leaky condition, the mate gave us a hat to bail with, and an oar to aid in steering. We then, supposing that he had in his boat as many as it could carry, proposed to steer for the shore. To this he replied that he would not quit the wreck until daylight, and that he would consider it an act of murder if he did. When we found that he had but five persons in his boat, we decided to cruise with him among the fragments of the wreck to pick up as many persons as his boat would carry. In our leaky state, we had as many on board as our boat could float with.

Following at a short distance, we continued for several hours to cruise among the wreckage, strewn over the sea, and which threatened in the darkness to stave in our frail barks. The mate directed his course as he heard the calls for assistance. The first person saved was Mr. Byrd of Georgia, who was nearly exhausted with the effort of supporting himself. The next were two firemen, dreadfully scalded. We were then hailed by some persons on a raft, who said they were 10 in number. Fearing that they would sink our boats, we turned away from them. The next person picked up was a young German, a son of the Duke of Leuchtenberg, who was found floating on a settee. The last was an old gentleman, Judge Rochester of New York.

The mate then came alongside and requested us to take the last gentleman into our boat, which we did. When he was turning off, the Judge, filled with joy at his escape, and gratitude to his preserver, called out in the most heart-felt manner, "Mr. Hibbert you are a noble fellow. God bless you!" Alas, at that moment of supposed safety, he little thought that he had received but a brief respite from that watery grave into which he was destined to sink, after enjoying for a few hours the cheerful light of day!

As both boats had now as many persons as they

could carry, it was proposed that we should direct our course for the land. Our longer stay near the wreck could be productive of no good to others, and might endanger our lives, should a change of wind or stormy weather occur. We were also desirous of avoiding the harrowing sight of recognizing our perishing friends, and of leaving them with a knowledge of who they were, without being able to render them any assistance. These reasons, added to the threatening appearance of the sky, from which a squall of wind and rain had just burst over us, over-ruled the objections of the mate, and at half past three oclock, the heads of the boats were turned towards the land.

The moon, which had risen about two hours before, gave but a feeble light behind a mass of heavy clouds; and the first faint streaks of morning light were just appearing in the East. Under a gloomy sky, the sea was heaving in long inky waves; the fragments of the wreck floated by us, but we saw nothing of the hull of the *Pulaski;* and we presumed, from its sudden disappearance from our eyes, and the assurance of those we had picked up, that it had sunk with the machinery. The only survivors were supposed to be those who were still clinging to fragments of the wreck, to whom we could render no further assistance; and with heavy hearts we turned away from the melancholy scene. The calls for aid were still heard around us. As they came faintly and despairingly from the distance, now drowned by the winds and waves, and again swelling mournfully in the air, the unseen spirits of the deep seemed to be waiting for the untimely fate of the young, the beautiful, the wise and the brave, whose lifeless but yet warm bodies were sinking to that deep tomb where rest the "sea buried."

The land was supposed to lie in a North-West direction, about 35 miles distant; and the mate, steering one boat, and myself the other, we struck off for it. Few words were exchanged; and in silence, broken only by the moans of the scalded firemen, one of whom was fast dying from the acuteness of his sufferings, we proceeded on our melancholy and dangerous voyage. The sea and wind were both high, but the boats, which had become tighter, rode the waves admirably, as they reeled on the crests or plunged into the deep gulfs between.

Day at length broke, and all eyes were directed to every point of the horizon, in the hope of seeing some friendly sail, but nothing met the sight but the boundless ocean, which seemed the more dreary and solitary when contrasted with the small and frail barks which were tossing on its bosom. The sun rose brilliantly, and the hearts of all were insensibly cheered. The heat however soon became oppressive, as it fell with tropical fervor on the unprotected heads of the half naked party; and such expedients as were in the power of each were adopted for protection. The ladies and children found the ample folds of the cloak almost as valuable a screen against the rays of the sun as it had proved against the chill wind of the night. The gentlemen resorted to handkerchiefs, waistcoats and aprons as substitutes for hats. The half clad and grotesque appearance of every one, tended to excite feelings of the ridiculous, which were suppressed as soon as they arose by the recollection of the awful scene that had just been witnessed, and by the danger yet before us. Notwithstanding this there was an obvious feeling of cheerfulness pervading the party. The mind, after the intense excitement of the night, required relief, and passed rapidly from a state of despair to that of hope. Conversation became general; and the ladies, who during the most trying period of the night, had never uttered an expression of fear, showed a calmness and cheerfulness that did them the greatest honour.

Directing our course by the position of the sun,

we continued to pull steadily for the shore. The only coat in the boat, was extended by two of the seats, and erected into a temporary sail. Aided by it, the oars, the waves and the wind, which blew directly on to the shore, we proceeded at the rate of three miles an hour.

The moaning of the scalded seamen increased as the day advanced; and it was a piteous sight to witness the swollen, blackened and skinless faces of the two poor wretches, as they writhed under the burning sun, and tossed their arms about in an agony of pain. About 9 o'clock the men in the mate's boat lay on their oars, and allowed us to pass ahead of them, until they were sufficiently astern to escape the observation of the ladies; when the body of one of the scalded men, who had died, was consigned to the deep. The boat then came alongside, and it was proposed to relieve us of some of our crew, as we were overloaded. Judge Rochester and the Negro women were accordingly transferred to it.

The men in the boats, taking their turns, now continued to row under a scalding sun, which blistered their faces, hands and feet, and occasioned a painful thirst. There being neither water nor food in the boats, the only relief to be found was in keeping the arms and feet wet with salt water.

About 10 o'clock a large shark came near the boats, but after some time left us.

The men, who had been exerting themselves incessantly since mid-night, now began to sink from fatigue and thirst; and every eye was anxiously directed toward land. Deceived by their wishes, there were frequent false reports. At last, about 12 o'clock, the mate, who was standing up in his boat, was observed to wave his handkerchief and point to the West. As we strained our eyes in that direction, a faint line of blue, hanging above the water, and scarcely distinguishable from it, gave us the glad assurance that we were really in sight of land. The hopes of the party revived, and with it their strength. Even the poor Negro, whose tongue had been for some time hanging from his mouth from exhaustion, cheered up and renewed his efforts.

As we neared the land it was found to be low, with a white sandy beach skirting it.

Deceived by our wishes, we imagined that we saw houses and villages; but they vanished from our sight as we approached, and melted into barren hillocks and a desert shore. At 3 o'clock we were within a quarter of a mile of the land, and endeavored to discover some inlet or bay which would afford us a safe landing. But as far as the eye could reach, there was between us and the land an uninterrupted wall of heavy breakers roaring and dashing on it with irresistible force.

Beyond the beach at a distance of two miles, the country appeared to be wooded; and in the midst of a field several buildings were distinguishable. Behind us was the ocean with all the recollections of the fearful night; before us the firm land, associated with the idea of perfect safety; but between us and that place of security dashed the breakers, threatening destruction to all who should attempt to reach it through them.

The mate, who was some distance in advance, laid on his oars until we came up. He then said that the men in his boat, worn out with fatigue, thirst and hunger, refused to row any farther, and had retermined to attempt a landing; but that he himself regarded it as a very dangerous measure. Fully agreeing with him, I urged the propriety of keeping down the coast, in the hope of reaching some inlet, or of meeting aid from the shore. Being overruled by the men in both boats, who insisted on landing at once, we most reluctantly consented to do so. Mr. Hibbert then proposed that as there were ladies and children on our boat, we should lie off until he made the attempt, when he would be prepared to point out the best course for us, and be ready to assist us as we reached the shore.

In pursuance of this advice our yawl was kept with her head to the sea, about 100 yards from the breakers, to await the result of the landing of the other boat. Every eye was fixed on her. We saw her rise to the summit of the first breaker, and disappear behind it. Anxiously we sought to catch a view of her rising on the crest of the next; but for some moments nothing was to be seen but the sheet of angry foam which extended for a hundred yards from the shore. It was now certain that she had upset, and that all in her were struggling for life in the boiling surf. In a short time two persons were seen issuing from the waves and reaching the shore. They turned after resting a few seconds, and entering the water, dragged two others to the shore, who were thrown on the beach, where they lay apparently insensible. The first two were then seen to walk in a hurried manner up and down the beach, again enter the water, and bring out another. After a considerable interval of time, the sixth was dragged to the shore. Those who had landed were then observed to spread themselves along the beach, as if searching for the remainder of their party, but no more appeared. After a time they were seen to drag their boat out of the water.   All further hope then ceased, and it was certain that five out of the eleven had perished. They were, as we afterward learned, Judge Rochester, Mr. Byrd, the scalded fireman and the two Negro women.

Deterred by the fate of the other boat, my companions now consented to keep off until they could receive aid from the shore through those who had just landed; but they positively refused to row any farther, as I earnestly urged them to do.   It was now but 3 oclock, and as the sun set after 7, we had still four hours of light; in which time, feeble and exhausted as we were, we could row, with the aid of the wind, 8 or 10 miles, in which distance there was every probability of finding some inlet or safer place of landing.   There was also the probability that the wind, which was blowing freshly from the South East, would subside at sun-set; or that a squall then forming over the land, would come out and enable us to run in with safety, when the first gust of wind should flatten the sea.   On men, suffering from intense thirst, and exhausted by fatigue, these arguments had however no influence. Exertion had become severely painful, and as long as there was the faintest hope of safety they were willing to encounter the danger before them.

To our signals of inquiry the men on shore replied by gestures not to be misunderstood that we should keep off and not attempt to land. In spite of this our men insisted on landing, and I was finally compelled to enter into a compromise with them, that when the sun touched the horizon, if no aid came to our relief, I would steer them to land.

The time dragged heavily along, as, with her bow to the sea, the boat was merely kept from drifting into the breakers; while we waited anxiously, but in vain, for the hoped for succor. The wished for squall, after rising for some time, was beaten back by the wind from the sea. The sun at last sunk behind the heavy mass of clouds that obscured the Western sky, and I proceeded to make such arrangements as promised to insure the safety of the helpless women and their children. Barney, the young sailor, as the person most to be relied on, was requested to save Mrs. Fraser, should we be upset. Solomon, the Negro man, was to take care of her child. At Mrs. Nightengale's suggestion, her infant was lashed to her by the folds of her shawl, and I was to endeavor to save them both. Having requested the ladies not to grasp any one around the neck who came to their assistance, and general instructions having been given to the party to advance rapidly as the breakers struck them, to stand still and brace themselves as they receded, and to recover if possible their footing, should they fall, I requested Barney and Solomon to prepare themselves by taking some rest in the bottom of the boat. Following their example, I instantly fell asleep for a quarter of an hour, when, being aroused, I again took the steering oar, whilst Barney and Solomon rowed.

The head of the boat was turned to the shore, and, waiting until the third heavy roller raised us on its crest, the order was given; and in an instant we were among the breakers, in a wide sheet of hissing and boiling foam. The boat darted forward with the velocity of an arrow, and the next instant the following wave dashed the oar out of the hands of the Negro, and before he could use that which I threw to him, the boat broached to. Another breaker came roaring behind, and hung with its curling crest over us, then rushed into the boat with the force of a cataract. In an instant the boat turned bottom up, and we were all thrown into the sea. I felt a severe blow on the back of my head, and another on my breast, and I found myself under the water with the boat above me. Holding my breath, I dove down, then struck off until the light was seen above, and then rose to the surface. The boat was floating a few yards from me, keel up, and beyond it the men who had just come to the surface, were swimming for the shore. Neither of the ladies were to be seen, but in a few seconds the back of Mrs. Fraser came slowly to the surface. Her head and feet were under water and she appeared to be struggling. As I rescued her and brought her head above water, I found she had her son grasped convulsively by the wrist. Reaching the boat, I supported the two across it, and called to Barney and Solomon, reminding them of their promise. They turned back at once, and I gave one to each, then looked for Mrs. Nightengale and her child. They were nowhere to be seen, and I was about to dive under the boat, thinking that they might be entangled there, when something brushed against my feet, and looking down I saw a body floating about three feet deep with the undertow out to sea. Diving down I caught Mrs. Nightengale by the hair and brought her to the surface. She was still conscious, and the infant was as composed as if resting in its nurse's arms. Supporting them with my right hand, I swam back to the boat, and held on to the keel with my left. In this situation we were forced toward the shore by the breakers. Feeling the bottom at last, I took Mrs. Nightengale by the arm, and we waded to the edge of the beach, where the men ashore assisted us.

The excitement being over, my strength suddenly failed me, and I fell, in an almost insensible state, on the sand. I had the happiness before I did so, of knowing that the ladies and their children, and every person belonging to our boat, were safely landed.

The rescued party finally reached Wilmington, where they were received with the utmost kindness, provided with clothes, and hospitably entertained. The next morning they had the pleasure of witnessing the arrival of thirty more of the *Pulaski* passengers, who had been picked up by a passing schooner from three fragments of the wreck, after drifting for four and a half days without water or food. Among them was Rhynah, Mrs. Nightengale's colored nurse. Eventually fifty-nine persons were saved from the doomed *Pulaski*.

Mr. Couper and his party proceeded to Norfolk and Baltimore, being franked the entire way, and here they were met by Mr. Rufus King of New York, the father of Mrs. Nightengale. Of the latter Mr. Couper wrote later, "Mrs. Nightengale behaved most heroically. Neither of the ladies uttered an exclamation of fear when death seemed inevitable. Had they lost their presence of mind, I could never have saved them."

After stopping in Philadelphia, Mr. Couper went on to New York, where he stayed with his best friend, Mr. John Lord, who was now at the head of his profession and had become a very wealthy man. While there he paid a visit to the Kings near Jamaica, Long Island, where a delegation from the community waited on him to thank him for the great service he had rendered "their valued fellow citizen and his family."

He was received by everyone with the utmost kindness and courtesy, and wrote his wife, "It is very well that you are not inclined to jealousy, for I assure you that I am much made of by the ladies at present. It is not often that any one is so well rewarded for the performance of a duty, as I have been in this instance."

X

BROUGHTON: THE RICE ISLAND

AMONG the many Carolina gentlemen who invested in the rich land along the Altamaha and adjacent coast was General Henry Laurens. Broughton, one of the smaller coast islands, was granted to him by South Carolina, and in 1760 he placed slaves on it and cleared the lands for rice planting. He was the first planter who used tidewater for irrigation, the backwaters of the land swamps having been used for this purpose before his time. After Laurens' death, William Brailsford of South Carolina bought Broughton Island.

William Brailsford was the only son of Samuel Brailsford, a merchant of London and Liverpool who did business with the Colonies, and of Susan Holmes of Charleston. William was educated in England, and grew up to be a gay young man who dressed in fine silks and laces, silk stockings and silver buckles, and who often visited Paris. After the Revolution a mercantile failure brought the family from England to Charleston, but their sympathies always remained with the English.

William Brailsford married Maria Hayward and had eight children, six of whom grew to maturity. When in Paris in his youth he had admired the silver forks he saw there, and he now imported six small forks for his children, and saw that they used them. He was very particular with their mental and physical training, and determined that all should grow up as straight as arrows. In 1802, after his purchase of Broughton Island, he moved all of the Negroes of his wife's estate to Georgia, coming with them to settle them on the island. He was courteously received by the coast families, and found congenial friends on St. Simon's.

Broughton, like Butler's Island, consisted of low rice fields intersected by ditches, the whole surrounded by an embankment. On the farthest point back the island was exposed to the sea, and the rice barn had been solidly built as a refuge in time of storms. Between this building and the plantation settlement flowed a deep broad canal, across which was a board and rail crossing for wagons.

In September 1804, a hurricane swept the Georgia coast. The overseer on Broughton had been directed to move the Negroes across the canal to the barn at the first approach of a storm. He was said to have been drunk, and the Negroes were not ordered to move until it was too late. Terrified at the violence of the storm, the Negroes tried to cross the canal in a flat, and eighty-five men, women, and little children were swept away, never to be seen again. It is said that the news of the disaster reached Mr. Brailsford in Charleston on the eve of a dinner party. He received and entertained his guests, and no one else knew of the calamity until the following day.

Then the direst distress prevailed in the house. The Charleston life was at an end, and the family decided to move to Broughton as soon as a rough house could be put up by plantation carpenters. Mr. Brailsford, with his oldest daughter, Elizabeth, went ahead of the family, and the two were entertained by Major Butler on St. Simon's until it was safe to go to Broughton. There they were joined by the rest of the family, and the advent of the young people was the first event that lifted the Negroes from despondency.

On Broughton Elizabeth Brailsford was married to Major Wood of Potosi Island, a Virginia gentleman and rice planter. She lived only a year, and died in McIntosh County, leaving no children. At almost the same time, Samuel, the oldest son, who had remained in Charleston, was killed in a duel by John Parker, both being in love with the same young lady, Anne Glover, a cousin of the Brailsfords.

With insufficient labor no crops could be grown on the island, and it is only natural that in the midst of so much adversity Mr. Brailsford was obliged to sell Broughton, which thus came into the possession of the Forman family of Savannah.

In time Broughton Island became the winter home of Mr. Thomas Forman, who had changed his name from Bryan at the request of his Grandfather Forman of Maryland. There were five children in his family, two boys and three girls — Hugh and Jack and Gussie, Carter and Georgia. The dwelling house, which stood on the embankment only about thirty yards from the river, was a two-storied house, built low on account of hurricanes, with four rooms on a floor. It was a pleasant place surrounded by orange trees, and immediately in front was the boat landing. The landing across the river was called "Holover," as visitors would call or halloo, and a boat would be sent across for them.

The little children loved the island, although the only place they could walk was along the embankments. What they especially delighted in was running across the many ditches and canals on boards thrown over them for the convenience of the Negroes.

On Broughton the Negroes' houses were built of logs, and stood on supports to avoid dampness. They consisted of two rooms divided by a good-sized hall, and each room had a large fireplace. The slaves had their own little patches of ground, and always kept chickens, selling poultry and produce to the family. The Negro women worked in the fields as well as the men, tying up their skirts with rope in a picturesque fashion. It was their custom to carry everything — bundles, baskets, or buckets — on their head, and, with hand on hip, to move with a swinging, graceful motion, always singing as they walked. They used a biggin in which to milk, a wooden pail with one stave longer than the rest for a handle, and this they also carried on their head full of milk, without spilling a drop. It was the ambition of the little white girls to walk as the Negroes did, with a weight on their heads.

Broughton was a rice island, and the garnered rice was carried from the fields to the flats, then towed to the mill, where it was threshed and loaded on ships to be carried to the city. The rice was not husked at the plantation mills. This was done in the city, as rice was not considered good in those days unless freshly beaten. On the plantation it was beaten fresh for dinner every day. For this purpose pestles and mortars, hewn from the trunks of trees, were used, these becoming smooth and shining like metal from constant use. Two boys or two women would seize the pestles together in the middle, raising and letting them fall so quickly and evenly that the beating of rice was not considered a difficult task. The children often tried to use the pestles, but never succeeded, as the motion required a knack they did not possess. After the rice was loosened from the husks, it was placed in flat-bottomed baskets called fanners, held high, and allowed to fall into baskets placed on the ground, the wind blowing the chaff away. This process, which was called "fanning the rice," was repeated until the rice was perfectly clean. The cooking of the rice was as important as its freshness, and the same result was achieved by cooking it in either cold or boiling water. In either case it was boiled for about fifteen minutes only, and afterwards steamed for about an hour, when each pearly grain was separate, enlarged and perfectly tender.

An old Charleston aristocrat once said of an up-countryman, "He told me they boiled their rice for an hour. That is all I want to know of that gentle-man." Certainly the blue glue served on many tables is not rice as the coast people know it.

The corn was ground on Broughton in the Bibli-cal manner, "two women grinding at the mill." Large stones, the upper with a hole in it, were con-nected by a pole with the roof of the shed in which they stood. The women would take hold of this pole and turn the stone with a celerity and ease that were surprising. "I can shut my eyes now at any time," Georgia Bryan Conrad wrote many years afterward, "and hear the whirring of the stones, the soft rustle of the meal as it fell in the basket placed to receive it, and the sound of the women's voices as they sang in the mill."

This sound of singing haunts the memories of all who were of that time and place, for, working in the fields, carrying their burdens as they walked, feeding the rice mill, or rowing on the river, the Negroes always sang — strange songs that were wild and melancholy and ineffably sweet.

Eight Negroes rowed the large and heavy boats in which the Forman family went back and forth to Darien. Sometimes it took two or three boats to hold them all, with their luggage and attendants.

When the tide was low and the channel through which they passed was narrow, the Negroes stood up and poled the boat. If the water was still too low to float it, they rolled up their pants, sprang overboard, and pushed until the boat reached deep water. The singing was as much a part of the performance as the rowing, and as soon as they were aboard again the song was taken up immediately. The children were always carried to and from the boat in the brawny arms of the oarsmen, and with their little arms around the men's necks they felt as safe and contented as possible. When the tide was low at the Broughton landing place even the older members of the family had to be carried ashore, and two Negroes would form what was called a "chair" with their hands, and carry them to land.

In winter the Negro men and women on Broughton wore stout linsey garments and heavy shoes and stockings, and the women always wore gayly colored bandannas on their heads. In summer a blue jean, now called denim, was substituted, which made serviceable garments, hard to tear and easy to patch. Mr. Forman thought it made the Negro women too helpless to have their clothes made for them, so the material was given to them to make their own, and a ragged slave was never seen on the Forman plantation. Blankets were given out every winter, those who had them one year not receiving them the next. The weekly rations consisted of bacon, rice, corn meal, hominy, and molasses. At harvest time and on holidays, tobacco was added. When beeves and sheep were killed on the place, the Negroes had a share. The waters teemed with fish, crabs, shrimp, and oysters, and in that rich rice mud vegetables grew abundantly. The Negroes had a way of throwing various things together into a pot and boiling them with a piece of bacon, which was particularly good.

No stoves were used in those early days. In the kitchens were large fireplaces, with cranes and hooks suspended, on which pots and kettles were hung. Tin "kitchens" were placed in front of the fire for roasting meat. Broilers were used over red-hot hickory coals, and bake ovens had lids for coals on top, so that bread and cake should be baked above as well as below. In addition to these there were long-handled toasters, and waffle and wafer irons.

When Maum Celie, the Formans' cook, baked corn wafers for dinner, she placed them in rows on boards laid on either side of the chimney, to keep them warm and crisp. Many were the times when the children would run in and beg for a hot corn wafer. Maum Celie, who was always kind, would take two wafers from her board, butter them, and hand them to the children in turn, who thought that nothing ever tasted better.

Broughton was noted for its lavish hospitality and its grand dinners, with fine-bred Southdown mutton and excellent wines. "But then," Charles Wylly writes, in 1920, "Volstead had not been born — damn him. He has not only taken away our wines and liquors, but he has made dining an impossibility. Now we only eat at our tables. In those days the best thoughts we had were reserved for the after-dinner talk, and many an interesting story have I heard as the decanters wandered over the table."

The planter of those days retained the habits of his Colonial progenitors and gave more attention to the etiquette of manner, dress, and of the table than is now required. The service at meals was more formal, and the ladies were always handed to their seats by the gentlemen.

The old slave was politeness personified, and the house servants, the men particularly, had a courtliness of manner borrowed from their masters that was striking. The women never entered a room without curtseying, and never seated themselves unless asked to do so, and they were as particular about the manners of their offspring as of those of the white children entrusted to their care. They were often heard saying, "Whar's yo manners?" "Show yo manners," or "I'll learn you yo manners." Little Georgia Forman was once at supper at the home of her uncle, Dr. Screven, of Savannah. He had a butler named William, a tall, solemn-looking individual, who was always immaculately dressed. Georgia was very fond of buttered toast, and had put out her hand for the last slice on the plate when William said to her in a low tone, "That belongs to Mr. Manners." Georgia stopped, horrified, supposing that Mr. Manners was a guest who had not yet been served. A little later, happening to pass the pantry door, she saw William calmly eating that identical slice of toast. Seeing her, he made a bow and said, "*I* am Mr. Manners." Another elegant butler belonged to the Virginia Bryans. When little Delia and a visiting cousin were laughing and dancing around the dining table before the family came in, he said loftily, "On-genteel, young ladies. On-genteel!" And the young ladies were crushed.

The Forman children were carried at stated times to visit their grandfather, Governor Troup, in middle Georgia, and after his death in 1856, continued to visit their aunt, who resided on her plantation,

Turkey Creek, the name of which she had changed to Valambrosa. Governor Troup died when Georgia was eleven, and left all of his property to the five Forman children. He owned six cotton plantations, and between six and eight hundred slaves, so, though a mere child, Georgia found herself the owner of a plantation and about ninety human beings. It gave her no feeling of exultation, and the responsibility weighed so upon her that when the slaves were finally freed, she said, "It was with a feeling of relief that the burden was laid down. Not that I think the way in which the slaves gained their freedom was justifiable. Far from it. I feel that the sudden manner in which they were freed was the greatest wrong ever done to any people, white or black. No one who was not on the spot can understand the suffering brought about by the severance of the old relations. If it had been done gradually, both the whites and blacks might have had time to adjust themselves to the new conditions."

The mother of the Forman children died when they were small, and later on their father married again and they went to Maryland to live. The three daughters were educated in Philadelphia, Baltimore, and Richmond, and when the war came on were sent down to spend the summer of '61 at

Montgomery, near Savannah. The oldest sister, their "leader and dear defender," died in this year, and only Gussie Bryan, the beauty of the family, and Georgia Forman were left. The latter married Mr. Holmes Conrad of Virginia, and spent the rest of her life in Winchester, Virginia, where her interesting and attractive daughters lived until recently.

The sweetness of Georgia Forman's character is shown in her little book of Memoirs, from which the foregoing facts are taken. To the end of her life she cared deeply for her faithful black friends, of whom she wrote, "As my dear black Mauma was the first to hold me on entering this world, so I trust that only black arms shall carry and lay me to rest in my last bed, on leaving it."

XI

FANNY KEMBLE

TWENTY-THREE years had passed since Major Butler had left St. Simon's Island, and the "Big House"
had fallen almost into ruins when, in the winter of
1838, Pierce Butler brought his wife and two little
daughters to the South. He was the grandson of
the old Major, and at his request had changed his
name from May to Butler. He had married
Fanny Kemble, the English actress, who had had
a brilliant stage career.

The portrait of Fanny Kemble by Lawrence is
that of a glorious beauty, but she is described by
one who met her as "an ugly little dark woman."
Perhaps the truth lies between the two. At any
rate she was a very gifted woman, gifted as a
writer as well as an actress.

Mr. Butler took his family first to his rice plantation on Butler's Island at the mouth of the Altamaha. This island lay below the level of the
river, being protected by an embankment. A double row of orange trees, planted on this, once

surrounded the entire island. Seeing these in full fruit and flower, Basil Hall declared it as well worth a trip to America to see as Niagara Falls. But the intensely cold winter of 1835 had destroyed these trees.

The only house on Butler's Island, besides the four "villages" in which the Negroes lived, and the three large tabby barns, was that of the overseer. In this small three-roomed house — in existence until recently — Mrs. Kemble, as she is usually called, spent the winter. The only walks she could take were along the embankment, the river on one hand, "a poisonous looking swamp on the other," beyond which were the low rice fields, divided into monotonous squares by dikes. In the thickets were bay, wild myrtle, and "the magnolia grandiflora, unrivalled in the whole vegetable kingdom," she writes. "Under these the spiked palmetto forms an impenetrable covert, while from branch to branch hang garlands of ever-green creepers, on which the mocking birds are singing and swinging even now in winter."

Fanny Kemble abhorred slavery, and should never have married a slave owner, for on that rock her marital happiness was wrecked. She kept a journal in the form of letters written to an Abolitionist friend in the North, Elizabeth Dwight

Sedgwick of Lenox, Massachusetts, and in these letters she gives a most painful account of slavery as seen on her husband's plantations. She expected and wished to see slavery from her own standpoint, and would consider no other side. The worthless class of Negroes on the plantation took advantage of her horror of slavery and made the most of their burdens to her. With their quick perception, they realized what it was she wanted to know, and they played easily upon her prejudices. They had real hardships to endure, which she saw with her own eyes, these being probably the result of absentee ownership, but the starvation rations she speaks of did not prevent the Butler Negroes from being strong, vigorous, and apparently happy. And far from being ignorant and debased, the testimony of other observers was that the Butler Negroes were the most intelligent in the community.

After the Civil War this Butler property was managed by James Maxwell Couper, a son of James Hamilton Couper, and he writes regarding the Negroes: "The labor consisted entirely of the slaves of former years of this place. I found them to be about the most intelligent, honest and industrious Negroes I have ever employed, and I have handled thousands of them. The mechanics were unusually intelligent and skillful for Negroes. Their loyalty to the memory of Major Butler and Pierce Butler, and their attachment to their old slave homes, was remarkable. If the conditions were such as pictured by Mrs. Kemble, it certainly is astonishing that after their emancipation I should have found such a feeling existing. Mrs. Kemble did the intelligent class of Negroes an injustice. *She did the same to the owner.*"

Fanny Kemble, believing the tales of overtasking, flogging, and heartless cruelty which were poured into her eager ears, was almost driven frantic, for she was a warm-hearted, sympathetic woman. Feeling that these poor helpless chattels were suffering the tortures of Dante's *Inferno,*— her own simile,—she suffered tortures herself, and came to hate everything and everyone in the South. Darien she considered "the abomination of desolation," and she loathed "the vapid conversation—with its slave slobber—of the women." The men she accused of "pride, profligacy, idleness, cruelty, cowardice and ignorance," and mentions "their ineffable abasement. Drinking, gambling and debauchery being their sole recreations."

Believing what she did, she cannot be blamed for writing, "The black history of oppression is laid before my eyes in this place, where there is the lowest of all civilized societies."

How the Abolitionist friend must have gloated over these letters!

The only thing on Butler's Island, apart from its natural beauty, with which Fanny Kemble was pleased was the "fragrant bath tubs made of cedar" by the Negroes on the place, which she preferred to "the finest Staffordshire porcelain."

When spring came Pierce Butler took his wife and two little daughters down to Hampton Point on St. Simon's Island. The main house being in a ruinous condition, they stayed in the house that had formerly been the overseer's. It stood within fifty feet of the bluff, and was old and in bad repair. In 1863, it was destroyed by the Federal troops. The foundations of this house can still be seen, though hard to find on account of a thicket of myrtles.

Fanny Kemble loved nature, and wrote enthusiastically of the beauty of St. Simon's. She rode on horseback through the cathedral aisles of its woods, and wrote, "You can not imagine anything so exquisite as the perfect curtains of yellow jessamine with which the whole island is draped. As the boat comes sweeping down toward the Point, the fragrance from the thickets, hung with their golden garlands, greets one, before one can distinguish them. It is enchanting."

Of spring on St. Simon's, she writes, "The
acacias are swinging their silver censers under the
green roof of these wood temples, and honeysuckles
twine around every tree. Beautiful butterflies
flicker like flying flowers among the bushes, and
gorgeous birds, like winged jewels, dart from the
boughs."

She writes of the strange birds in the swamps,
of the crane, ibis, and eagle, and gives two beautiful pictures of her impressions at night in this far
Southern home.

"We drove home by moonlight, and as we came
towards the woods in the middle of the island, the
fireflies glittered out from the dusky thickets, as
if some magical golden veil was every now and
then shaken out into the darkness. The air was
enchantingly mild and soft, and the whole way
through the silvery night, delightful."

And again, "Last night I went out into the air
to refresh my spirits. The scene beyond the house
was beautiful. The moonlight slept on the broad
river, which is here almost the sea, and on the
masses of foliage of the great Southern oaks. The
golden stars shone in the purple curtains of the
night, and the measured roar of the Atlantic upon
the white sands of the beach of Long Island, re-
sounded through the air."

"I should like the wild savage loneliness," she continues, "if it were not for slavery." And one can sympathize with her, believing what she did. She found St. Simon's as depressing as Butler's Island, and felt she would die if she had to live among such savages. "I feel a weight of horror and depression," she wrote, "surrounded by all of this misery and degradation. It is impossible to conceive a more savage existence within the pale of civilization. The Southern aristocracy, thanks to the pernicious influences by which they are surrounded, are unfit to be members of a Christian republic."

What the Southern aristocracy thought of Fanny Kemble is not known. Not one of them would ever have put into print a personal criticism. On St. Simon's they all called politely, and she rode over the island returning their visits. Of old Frederica she says, "In the afternoon I drove down to visit old Mrs. Armstrong. . . . Hers and one other house are the only dwellings remaining in this curious wilderness of dismantled, crumbling grey walls, compassionately cloaked with a thousand profuse and graceful creepers."

Fanny Kemble attended service at the little church, "in its wild and beautiful situation, with magnificent live-oaks around it," and mentions the picturesque though sadly neglected burial ground. She was shocked by the lack of dignity in the service. "There was not even a clerk," she writes. Why the venerable "clark" and the estimable pew opener were not present is not known. Charles Wylly suggests that it may have been at this time that the grandchildren of the pew opener used her wooden leg as a back log for the fire. He acknowledges, however, the informality existing in his own day, when, as a child, he saw the rector cutting a melon in the vestry, when he should have been changing his vestments; and tells how the children of his own family sat on the floor of the pew, and opened their lunch baskets when the litany began. "There, hidden from view by the high pews, we were duly thankful for the mercies granted us, generally in the form of buttered waffles."

Mrs. Kemble wore to church an irreproachable London riding habit, which she contrasts with "the quaint and original costumes" she saw there. "The curious specimens of the art of dressing," she writes, "gradually distributed themselves among the two or three indescribable machines drawn up under the beautiful oak-trees, in which they departed in various directions to the several plantations on the island."

In the whole of Fanny Kemble's *Journal*, she has

kind words only for the Couper family. Of Mr.
John Couper, then eighty, she writes: —

After our return home, we had a visit from
Mr. Couper, one of our neighbors, an intelligent
and humane man, to whose account of the qualities
and characteristics of the slaves, as he had observed
and experienced them, I listened with great interest.

Our neighbor, Mr. Couper, and his family reside
entirely the year round on their plantation on St.
Simon's, without apparently suffering in their
health from the effects of the climate.   When the
heat is intense, the breeze from the ocean and the
salt air, I suppose, prevent it from being intoler-
able or hurtful. . . .

As an accompaniment to 'de beautifulest mutton
de Missus eber see,' we have just received from our
neighbor, Mr. Couper, the most magnificent supply
of fresh vegetables, green peas, salad, etc.   He
has a garden, and a Scotchman's real love for horti-
culture, and I profit by them in this very agreeable
manner. . . .

I must tell you of my visit to my neighbor, Mr.
Couper, which pleased and interested me very much.
He is an old Glasgow man, who has been settled
here many years.   It is curious how many of the
people round this neighborhood have Scotch names ;
it seems strange to find them in the vicinity of a
new Darien.   Mr. Couper's home is a roomy, comfortable, handsomely laid out mansion, to which
he received me with very cordial kindness, and

where I spent part of a very pleasant morning, talking with him, hearing all he could tell me of the former history of Mr. Butler's plantation. His description of its former master, Major Butler, interested me very much. . . . Old Mr. Couper spoke with extreme kindness of his own slaves, and had evidently bestowed much humane and benevolent pains upon endeavors to better their conditions. . . . He showed me his garden from whence came the beautiful vegetables he had more than once supplied me with. In the midst of it was a very fine and flourishing date-palm tree, which, he said, bore its fruit as prosperously here as it would in Asia. After the garden we visited a charming, nicely kept poultry yard, and I returned home much delighted with my visit and the kind good humor of my host. . . .

In the afternoon I rode with Mr. Butler, and wound up with a visit to dear old Mr. Couper, whose nursery and kitchen garden are a refreshment to my spirits. How completely the national characteristics of the worthy canny old Scot are stamped on the care and thrift visible in his whole property, the judicious successful culture of which has improved and adorned his dwelling in this remote corner of the earth! The comparison, or rather contrast between himself and his quondam neighbor, Major Butler, is curious enough to contemplate. The Scotch tendency of the one to turn everything to good account, the Irish propensity of the other to leave everything to ruin, disorder and neglect. The careful economy and prudent management of the mercantile man, the reckless profusion of the soldier. The latter made a splendid fortune, and spent it in Philadelphia, where he built one of the finest houses that existed in the old fashioned days. The other has resided here on his estate, ameliorating the condition of his slaves and his property, a benefactor to the people and the soil alike, a useful and good existence, an obscure and tranquil one. But it must not be forgotten that on the estate of this wise and kind master, a formidable conspiracy was once organized among his slaves.

Of Mrs. John Fraser, whose husband now had charge of Hamilton, Mrs. Kemble writes, "She is a kind hearted and intelligent woman, and a Lady Bountiful," and she tells of the fine mutton, magnificent prawn, fruit, and flowers sent by her on more than one occasion.

Fanny Kemble was on St. Simon's when the wreck of the *Pulaski* occurred, and read the letter written by James Hamilton Couper. In her *Journal*, she writes: —

I have just finished reading, with the utmost interest and admiration, James Couper's narrative of his escape from the wreck of the *Pulaski*. What a brave, gallant and unselfish soul he must be! You never read anything more thrilling, in spite of the perfect modesty of this account of his. The quiet unassuming character of his usual manners and deportment, adds greatly to his prestige as a hero. What a fine thing to be such a man!

You can not imagine how strikingly throughout this whole narrative the extraordinary power of Mr. Couper's character makes itself felt. The immediate obedience that he obtained from women, whose terror might have made them unmanageable, and men, whose selfishness might have defied his control. The wise though painful firmness which enabled him to order the boat away from the side of the perishing vessel, in spite of the pity that he felt for so many, in attempting to succor whom, he could only have jeopardized the few whom he was bound to save.

The firmness, courage, humanity, wisdom and presence of mind, all these admirable traits are miserably transmitted to you by my imperfect account; and when I assure you that his own narrative was as simple, modest and unpretending as it was interesting and touching, I am sure that you will agree with me that he must be a very rare man. When I spoke with enthusiasm to his old father of his son's noble conduct, and asked him if he was not proud of it, his sole reply was, "I am glad, Madam, my son was not selfish."

I have often written you of the disastrous effects of slavery upon the character of the white men implicated in it. Many among themselves feel and acknowledge it to the fullest extent, and no one

more than myself, can deplore that any human
being I love should be subject to such baleful influences, but the devil must have his due, and men
brought up in the habit of peremptory command
over their fellow men, and under the constant apprehension of danger, and awful necessity of immediate readiness to meet it, acquire qualities,
precious to themselves and others in the hour of
extreme peril, such as this man passed through,
saving by their exercise himself and all committed
to his charge.

It would seem that a society capable of producing such a man could hardly be "the lowest of all
civilized societies," and those who belonged to it
"unfit to be members of a Christian republic."

James Hamilton Couper did not approve of slavery himself, but he was forced to use the only labor
that could stand the deadly climate of the rice lands,
and he was as just and humane a master as his
father.

Public opinion frowned on an unkind master in
the South, and the cruel master was abhorred.
Mere self-interest prompted and in a measure enforced sufficient food, clothing, and shelter for the
slave. But with the absentee ownership that gradually came about, with wealth and extravagance,

the slave became but a chattel, and the subject race
was committed to a hired substitute, often chosen
from a class unworthy of trust.

It was Charles Wylly's opinion that there was
"no feature in the institution of slavery that did
not work far more injury to the white man than to
the black. It was difficult for the old not to grow
intolerant and domineering, and it caused extravagance and encouraged idleness in the young. In
some cases it even perverted justice by the spectacle
of a coming debacle, in which all might be losi.
Twice in my life I have known the Spectre to appear, to silence speech and stifle even thought, and,
after a day's reign, vanish. And in one case the
provocation was very great. But for those two
instances, I can truthfully say I know of no cruelty
that was practised on the slaves of the Georgia
coast."

Fanny Kemble left the South the following
spring, and never returned. Her diary was published in book form, and a new edition was brought
out by Henry Ward Beecher during the Civil War
for propaganda purposes.

In 1890, Mr. James Dent of Hofwyl Plantation,
and Mrs. Joseph Wilder of Savannah, who had
been Georgia King of St. Simon's, were visiting

Mrs. Leigh in England. Mrs. Leigh's mother, Mrs. Fanny Kemble Butler, was staying with her.

In answer to a letter from a friend, Mr. Dent wrote the following: —

I have your letter, and take great pleasure in repeating Mrs. Kemble's remarks. They were a great surprise to me, and I have no doubt were entirely sincere on her part. She had always interested me greatly. I had read her books and always thought, though she was doubtless often misled by Negroes' tales, that she always told what she *believed* to be true, and if there were errors, they were not hers.

I was a visitor at a small village where Mrs. Leigh was spending the summer, near London, and Mrs. Kemble was living with her daughter. I went down for dinner rather early, and found Mrs. Kemble in the drawing-room, and entered into conversation with her. It was in 1890, and the Force Bill was being agitated and causing some excitement. She said that she hoped the passing of this bill would not cause any violence in the South, and then said, "I suppose the South will never forgive me for what I wrote about slavery." I had to say *something,* so I said the South had come to realize the attitude of the world on the subject in late years, which was the best I could do. Of course I knew she was not forgiven. Then she said what so interested and surprised me.

"I was a young and passionate woman. I have

bitterly regretted many things I wrote in that book. I do not mean to say that my attitude on the subject of slavery has changed. That is the same. But when I think of the awful results of the war to those who were dear to me, I have much to be sorry for."

Mrs. J. H. Wilder was in the house, and I repeated the conversation to her as soon as I had an opportunity after dinner. She did not appear to be surprised, from which I infer that Mrs. Kemble had so expressed herself previously, but that is my inference only.

I have just read the first volume of Mrs. Kemble's *Journal,* written in 1832, when she first came to this country. She had not met *Mr. Butler,* or come South, and she says nice things of *us!* I enjoyed it. I am afraid the two events underscored caused a change of view, tho' she really did say many nice things, especially of James Hamilton Couper, and to this she alluded in the conversation.

Mrs. Joseph Wilder writes of the same visit: —

I am glad to tell you of my conversation with Mrs. Kemble in London. She called to take me to Westminster Abbey, and led me to where the tickets were given, saying she could have special cards from Dean Stanley, but so many Americans asked for them, she preferred to go with the crowd.

While we stood waiting for our turn, she said, "Will you follow a Northern leader?"

"I will follow *you,* Mrs. Kemble," I said.

"Oh!" she answered, "I wonder my husband had not *strangled* me — I was a fanatic."

I have never read her book. Mrs. Leigh, her daughter, said to me once she had never read it, for if she had she was afraid she would "hate" her mother. Her sympathies were altogether with her father.

You say that things were "horrible" as described by Mrs. Kemble. I stand strongly against such a statement. I know personally of two generations — my parents' and my own — with intimate traditions of my noble grandparents, and I knew and saw nothing "horrible."

It was without doubt, as I have often heard General Jackson say, the gentlest condition between Capital and Labor that has ever existed.

My father never allowed severe punishment, and was idolized by his people, and my mother was indeed a "Mother" to them. Wearing out her life in personal care of them. Taking care of the sick, comforting them in trouble, making ready good clothing and helpful medicines. Doing everything as the true mistress or friend.

I recall one woman who came to see us after she was free, who said, "Missus was our Mother. One night after 11 o'clock, she came out to the hospital with a fan for me, and said, 'The night is so hot, I thought you would need this.'"

A little thing, but showing loving-kindness.

Which view was nearer the truth? That of Fanny Kemble Butler, who spent one year in the South, or that of Georgia King Wilder, who spent a lifetime?

XII

HOPETON

In 1805, John Couper and his partner, James Hamilton, bought from David Deas and Arthur Middleton the tracts on the Altamaha shore which they called Hopeton, after their friend and financial backer, William Hopeton. This plantation was situated on the south bank of the river, about eight miles from Darien by water and sixteen from Brunswick by land. Not a foot of land was at that time cleared, so they placed large forces of Negroes on it, under the direction of overseers, and the rich swamp land was soon reclaimed. There were 4500 acres, 2500 being of pines, useless save for fuel and timber. Cotton was at first planted, then sugar cane, and finally rice became the staple crop. The plantation was worked by six hundred slaves or more.

In 1816, as has been said, James Hamilton Couper, the oldest son of John Couper, was given entire charge of Hopeton. He was at this time twenty-three years old. So well did the young man manage the Hopeton plantation that by 1825 it was acknowledged a model place. It was in this year that he went to Europe to study the diking system of Holland with the hope of improving the ditching of his rice fields.

The house at Hopeton had been originally the old plantation sugar house, and was a large substantial three-storied building of tabby. A broad flight of steps in front led up to the second story, on which were the drawing-room, library, study, and dining room. The drawing-room opened at the back on to a circular, uncovered porch, with curving steps leading down into the flower garden and shrubbery. The approach to the house was through an avenue of great live oaks, kept scrupulously clean by a set of little darkies who, under the direction of an old Negro woman, swept it every day with brooms made of brush.

James Hamilton Couper was as ardent a horticulturist as his father, and every flower and shrub that grew in those parts bloomed on his grounds.

Being the most methodical of men, every hour of the day was devoted to a certain duty. He rose at six, took a cold bath, shaved, dressed, and was in his study by seven. After breakfast he received his head men, and devoted the morning to plantation affairs. From two to four he was in his library reading or writing alone. At 4.15 to the minute he waited the appearance of the family and guests in the drawing-room, and after dinner, following a little conversation, he retired again to his study. For years he kept the most perfect plantation records, his books, neatly written, and beautifully illustrated with colored maps of Hopeton, showing the diversification of the crops each year. By this systematic use of his time he was able to cultivate his scientific tastes, and his correspondence was solicited by many learned societies. He was the leading conchologist of the South, and, as a microscopist, his researches into the new field of germ life attracted attention in the laboratories of many universities. He collected at great cost a library in which there was hardly any valuable work of the day found wanting — the first large edition of Audubon's *Birds of America,* Boidell's *Shakespeare,* Napoleon's *Egypt,* Sylvester's *Paleography,* and many volumes of engravings of the European galleries being among them. Through the Reverend Mr. Bartow, who had married his youngest sister, Isabella, he bought many paintings in Europe, most of them copies of the old masters, according to the taste of the day, and he had also a large collection of fine steel engravings.

When Mr. James Hamilton of Philadelphia died,

HOPETON ON THE ALTAMAHA
(Painted by John Lord Couper)

all of his large holdings in Georgia were inherited by his only daughter, who had married Mr. Richard Corbin of Virginia.   Mr. Couper administered her estate with his own for over forty years, becoming, at her death, the guardian of her son Richard and two daughters. Under his management Hopeton throve: he increased the acreage, made enormous crops, and, by skillful diking and ditching, almost eliminated the element of uncertainty, the bane of the coast planter.

J. D. Legare, editor of the *Southern Agriculturist* of Charleston, wrote in 1832: "Hopeton is decidedly the best plantation we ever visited, and we doubt whether it can be equalled in the Southern States.   When we consider the extent and variety of the crops, the number of operatives, who have to be directed and managed, it will not be presumptive to say it may fairly challenge comparison with any establishment of the United States, for the systematic arrangement of the whole, the regularity and precision with which all operations are carried out, and the perfect and daily accountability established in every department."

The Reverend George F. Clarke, pastor of the church at Carteret's, which was in the Hopeton parish, wrote from the North many years later, "My charge contained five white families and 1000 slaves. My evenings were delightful. Not only delightful but instructive. My host Mr. Couper, at Hopeton, was a man of most uncommon ability and attainment. His library was the largest and best selected I have ever seen in private ownership. I was acquainted with the more cultivated class of Southerners. They had inherited their slaves from their fathers or grandfathers, who had bought them from merchants of Boston or Newport. I saw no cruelty, and the servants did not work so hard as the wives of our Northern farmers." And he adds, "I wonder how many wealthy men of this day, would rise from their dinner tables to shake the hand of an aged servant, a sight I once witnessed at Hopeton."

In 1833, Mr. Couper extended his activities, and built the first cotton-seed oil mills, one near Mobile, and the other at Natchez, Mississippi. The first he put in charge of his brother John, and the second of his brother-in-law, John Wylly. Had he been able to manage them himself, they might have been successful, but under the circumstances he shared the fate of most pioneers, and by 1836 had to abandon the enterprise at a considerable loss.

By this time so well known had the Hopeton plantation become that no traveler of note who came South failed to visit it.

On his second trip to America, Sir Charles
Lyell, the distinguished English geologist, became a
guest at Hopeton, in January 1846. He writes: —

At the end of a long day's sail, our steamer landed
us safely at Darien, on the sandy banks of the Altamaha. . . . The next morning we were joined
by Mr. James Hamilton Couper, with whom I had
corresponded on geological matters, and whom I
have already mentioned as the donor of a splendid
collection of fossil remains to the Museum at Washington, and of other like treasures to that of Philadelphia. . . . Mr. Couper came down the river
to meet us in a long canoe, hollowed out of the trunk
of a single cypress, and rowed by six Negroes, who
were singing loudly, and keeping time to the strokes
of their oars. He brought us a packet of letters
from England which had been sent to his house,
a welcome New Year's gift, and when we had
glanced over the contents, we entered the boat, and
began to ascend the Altamaha.

The river was fringed on both sides with tall
canes, with the cypress and many other trees,
which, being hung with grey moss, gave a sombre
tone to the scenery, in spite of the green leaves of
several species of laurel, myrtle and magnolia.
Wherever there was a break in the fringe of trees,
a forest of ever-green pines was seen in the back-
ground. For many a mile we saw no habitation,
and the solitude was profound; but our black oarsmen made the woods echo to their song. Darien

is on the left or northern bank of the Altamaha.
About eight miles above it on the opposite bank,
we came to Hopeton, the residence of Mr. Couper,
having first passed from the river into a canal,
which traversed the low rice fields. Here we put
up prodigious flights of the marsh black-birds.
From the rice grounds we walked up a bank to a
level table-land above the river, covered with pines
and scrub oak. Here, in this genial climate, there
are wild flowers in bloom every day of the year.
On this higher level stands the house of Hopeton,
where we spent our time very agreeably for a fortnight. Much has been said in praise of the hospitality of the Southern planter, but they alone who
have travelled in the Southern States, can appre-
ciate the perfect ease and politeness with which a
stranger is made to feel himself at home. Horses,
carriages, boats, servants, are all at his disposal.
Even his little comforts are thought of, and everything is done as heartily and naturally as if no
obligations were conferred. The sacrifices made
by the planter are small, since he has a well trained
establishments of servants, and his habitual style
of living is so free and liberal, that the expense
of a few additional inmates is scarcely felt. Still
there is a warm and generous character in the
Southerners, which mere wealth and a retinue of
servants can not give.

A few days after our arrival, that is Jan. 4th,
1846, Mr. Couper took us in a canoe down the river,
from Hopeton to one of the sea islands called St.

Simon's, fifteen miles distant, to visit his summer
residence, and to give us an opportunity of explor-
ing the geology of the coast and adjoining low
country. On our way we landed on Butler's Island. The banks of the river here are adorned
with orange trees, loaded with golden fruit and
very ornamental. The Negro houses were neat
and white-washed, all floored with wood, each with
an apartment called the hall, two sleeping rooms
and a loft for the children.

We landed at the north-east end of St. Simon's,
called Cannon's Point. We found Mr. Couper's
villa near the water's edge, shaded by a verandah
and a sago tree. There were also many lemon
trees, somewhat injured by the late frost, but the
olives, of which there is a fine grove here, were
unharmed. We also admired five date palms,
which bear fruit. They were brought from Bus-
sora in Persia, and have not suffered by the cold.
The oranges have been much hurt. Some of the
trees, planted by Oglethorpe's troup in 1743, after
flourishing for 93 years, were cut off in February 1835.

I went with Mr. Couper to Long Island, the
outermost barrier of land between St. Simon's and
the ocean, four miles long. On the sea beach we
gathered no less than 29 specimens of marine shells.

During a fortnight's stay at Hopeton we had an
opportunity of seeing how the planters live in the
South, and the condition and prospects of the Negroes on a well managed estate. We visited the

hospital, which consists of three separate wards, one for men, another for women, and one for lying-in women. The latter are always allowed a month's rest after confinement. The hospital is in charge of the mistress of the plantation or the overseer's wife, assisted by a Negro woman, whose especial task is to look after the sick. The Negroes refuse to take medicine from any hands other than those of their master or mistress. When a Negro child is sick, it is usually the mistress who sits up all night, giving medicines, rather than the mother.

The Negro houses at Hopeton are as neat as the greater part of the cottages in Scotland. In each was a chest, a table, two or three chairs, and a few shelves for crockery. The Hopeton plantation children had such bright happy faces, and such frank confiding manners, as to be very engaging.

The relation of slaves to their masters resembles nothing in the Northern states. There is hereditary regard, and often attachment on both sides, more like that formerly existing between lords and their retainers, than anything now to be found in America. When his mechanics came to consult Mr. Couper on business, their manner of speaking to him was quite as independent as that of English artisans to their employers.

The responsibility of the owners is felt to be great, and to manage a plantation with profit, is no easy task; so much judgment is required, and such a mixture of firmness, forbearance and kindness.

I had many opportunities while here of talking with
the Negroes alone, or seeing them at their work.
I may be told that this was a favorable specimen of
a well managed estate; if so I may at least affirm
that mere chance led me to pay this visit, that is to
say scientific objects, wholly unconnected with the
'domestic institutions,' of the South, or the character of the owner in relation to his slaves. I can
but relate what passed under my own eyes, or what
I learned from good authority.

Sir Charles Lyell mentioned that "on the Hopeton plantation above 20 violins have been silenced
by the Methodist missionaries." A most unfortunate result of religious instruction, when we consider the Negro's passionate love of music and
his undoubted talent.

At Hopeton Mr. and Mrs. Couper raised a family of six sons and two daughters, all but one of
whom grew to maturity. Tutors from the North
were engaged to teach the sons, and governesses to
teach the daughters. Like their father, all of the
children were talented, John, the second son, being quite a gifted artist. The oldest son, Hamilton, and the youngest, Robert, also drew and
painted well. Margaret, the oldest daughter, kept
an album, after the fashion of the day, filled with
charming sketches by her brothers, which is still
treasured by her children. The lives of these

young people must have been ideally happy. Some
of them were students and all of them were readers,
and their father saw that they had every possible
opportunity for culture, while their mother, gentle,
affectionate, and sympathetic, made their home as
delightful as possible.

They were all devoted to their old grandfather,
and often visited him at Cannon's Point. The boys
found him especially congenial. He was literally
"one of them," and if, when they were having a
hilarious time together, the dignified James Hamilton Couper appeared, their grandfather would
say, "Behave yourselves, boys. Here comes *the
old gentleman!*"

At eighty he wrote to his oldest grandson, Hamilton, as follows: —

ST. SIMON'S 14 *March* 1839.

MY DEAR HAMILTON,

I should have been to Hopeton before this but
have been quite lame for some time. . . . I stag-
gered out this forenoon to give Old Harry — not
Old Nick, but old Parson Harry — direction to
prepare land for melons — and I look forward to
sending Mr. Dutton some cartloads for his good
boys, if he can find any amongst you — the bad
boys can scrape the rhinds — and good enough for
them. . . . Tell Aleck and John I will send them
each some melons with their name thereon.

If you have any Chinkoppin switches *to spare* send me some down for your cousin John Fraser. ... Make my respects and compliments to Mr. Dutton, and tell him to remember Solomon's wisdom.

I am my dear Hamilton your affectionate Grandfather,

JOHN COUPER.

In May 1851, Fredrika Bremer, the Swedish novelist, visited Hopeton, of which she wrote: —

Mr. Couper is one of the greatest planters in the United States, and this created in me a desire to become acquainted with him and his plantations. But I did not find him a reformer, merely a disciplinarian, with great practical tact, and also some benevolence in the treatment of Negroes.

In other words I found him to be a true representative of the gentlemen of the Southern States — a very polite man — possessing as much knowledge as an encyclopedia, and interesting to me in a high degree, through the wealth and fascination of his conversation. He is distinguished for his knowledge of natural history, has a beautiful collection of the natural productions of America, and the lecture which I heard him read this morning, in the midst of these, on the geology and rock formation of the world, has given me a clearer knowledge of the geological structure of this portion of the world than I ever possessed before.

In urbanity and grace of conversation Mr. Couper reminds me of Ralph Waldo Emerson, but in a general way, the Southern gentleman has too small a development of the organ of ideality, even as in the gentleman of the North it is too large.

The last distinguished visitor to Hopeton was the Honorable Amelia Murray, Lady in Waiting to Queen Victoria. In her *Letters from the United States* she writes: —

At last at night we reached Darien. Fortunately a four-oared canoe-like boat of Mr. Hamilton Couper's, had come down from his plantation up the Altamaha upon some business. We met Mr. Couper, and after a very pleasant row of about five miles, he brought us to his English-like house (as respects the interior) and interesting home, my first introduction to plantation life. A happy attached Negro population surrounds this abode; I never saw servants in any old English family more comfortable or more devoted; it is quite a relief to see anything so patriarchal after the apparently uncomfortable relations of masters and servants in the Northern States. I should much prefer being a "slave" here, to a grumbling, saucy "help" there! But every one to their tastes.

We left the river about a quarter of a mile from the house, and came up a narrow canal between rice plantations almost to the door; we passed two or three large flat-boats, laden with rice; and

Mr. Couper took me to see the threshing machine which was at work in the barn; the women putting in the rice just as we do our grain. They were more comfortably dressed than our peasantry, and looked happier; otherwise, except the complexions, the scene was much of the same kind as that at a threshing barn in England.

It is in vain to intend keeping silence upon the one thought that must be uppermost in a mind accustomed from childhood to erroneous views upon the slavery question, and I may as well write on. I now see the great error that we have committed is in assuming that the African race is equal in capacity with the European; and that under similar circumstances it is capable of equal moral and intellectual culture. . . . I believe the Negro race is incapable of self government; and I suspect its present condition in the United States is practically the best that the character of the Negro admits of. It is for their happiness and interest to remain in tutelage, at any rate for two or three generations.

Is there any part of Africa, the West Indies, or South America where three million of Negroes are to be found as comfortable, intelligent and religious, or as happy as in the Southern States? The most practical mode of improving a semi-barbarous race is to place it in the proportion of one to two in the midst of a civilized people. . . . There are of course painful exceptions to the generally kind and just rule of Southern planters, but they are the exceptions.

I went yesterday through a forest of Pirius Palustris to a spot where it is Mr. Couper's intention to build a house which is to be called Altama. It will be beautifully situated on the edge of a pine barren, a sloping thicket of live-oaks, magnolias and fan palms on one side, ending in rice plantations, with distant forest and river views extending toward Darien. The place was once the site of an Indian village, and I picked up fragments of their pottery.

I forgot to mention that there are from three to four hundred Negroes on this estate. Mr. and Mrs. Couper have no white servants. I should not like to inhabit a lonely part of Ireland or even Scotland, surrounded only by 300 Celts. I believe there is not a soldier or policeman nearer than Savannah, a distance of sixty miles.

Feb. 14th, 1855.

After the sharp white frost of Monday, we had rain yesterday, and the folks here hope winter has taken its departure. I can not find myself dull with this pleasant family. Yesterday we did all sorts of things, just as I would have done among my own belongings in England. We cooked, and drew, and studied natural history.

Such is the Negroes' feeling towards their masters that in some cases where freshets have put his crops in danger, they have worked freely 18 hours out of the 24, and for three weeks, to save them. The thanks of Mr. Couper, and a few little presents, make them quite happy. . . . The Creator of us formed them for labor under guidance, and there is probably a Providential intention of producing some good Christian men and women among them. We have been blindly endeavoring to counteract this intention, believing ourselves more religious, virtuous and benevolent than these slave holders. . . . I must tell of my honest convictions, and the *truth*. . . .

Mr. Couper will go with me to Brunswick, where the *St. John* steamer calls on her way to Palatka.

Because of her views on the question of slavery, Miss Murray found herself in disgrace on her return to England, and lost the position she had held at court.

The Altama house which Miss Murray mentions was built to be Mrs. Couper's dower house, but was only used by the family for a few years before the Civil War. It was a large, comfortable square house, built of tabby and painted orange color, and surrounded by the dark, glossy leaves of lemon and orange trees.

All visitors to Hopeton were struck by the melodious singing of the Negroes as they rowed up and down the Altamaha. It was the same all along the coast, where the singing was as much a part of the performance as the rowing. The Negroes improvised as they sang, each set trying to outdo the others, and never singing the songs of another plantation.

Fanny Kemble speaks of this in her Memoirs: —

Rowing yesterday evening through a beautiful sun-set into a more beautiful moon-rise, my two sable boat-men entertained themselves and me with alternate strophe and anti-strophe of my personal attractions. Sarah comes in for endless glorification on account of the brilliant beauty of her complexion. The other day our poets made a diversion from the personal to the moral qualities of their small mistress, and after the usual tribute to her roses and lilies, came the following rather significant couplet: —

Little Miss Sally.
That's a ruling lady.

At which all the white teeth simultaneously lightened from the black visages, whilst the subject of this equivocal commendation sat surveying her sable dependents with infantile solemnity.

Many of the old *ante bellum* boat songs have come down to the present day, and are still sung by the coast Negroes.

In 1857, Mr. Couper gave a house party at Hopeton as a farewell celebration. For forty years he had managed the Hopeton plantation; now he was about to give up his position as trustee for the estate of James Hamilton, the youngest of his three wards, Richard Corbin, Jr., having reached his majority. He had obtained letters dismissing the trusteeship, and had bought of Constance Corbin de Montmart the lands now called Altama and Carrs' Island, and had purchased from her sister the Hamilton plantation on St. Simon's Island, and a hundred and eighty Negroes. Mr. Couper now proposed to resign his management of Hopeton, recommend his brother, William Audley Couper, as his successor, and retire to Altama to devote his energies to his own affairs.

The number of guests was large, including two Englishmen—a Mr. Cavendish, M. P., and his traveling companion, Major Devereux, of the Horse Guards. Margaret Couper and three of her brothers were now grown, so there were a number of young people. Carrie Elliott, the beauty, and her charming sister Mary came with Sarah Berrien from Savannah, and there was also Miss Clinch, afterward Mrs. Heyward, of Camden County. The young gentlemen were Robert Stiles and Duncan Twiggs of Savannah, Wyatt Dickson of Augusta, and Hugh Bryan of Broughton Island. A Mr. Ballard, Charles Wylly, and

Fannie Fraser were also there. The young ladies considered Mr. Cavendish rather stupid, and Major Devereux bright but pert. At Broadfield, a nearby plantation, the Misses Fannie and Georgia Cohen were visiting the Troups, and dinners and teas were exchanged.

In spite of the number of guests, the systematic routine of Mr. Couper's life was not altered. He was closing up an account of a forty-year stewardship, entailing the balancing of thousands of dollars in expenditure, receipts, losses, and gains, all to be placed in their respective columns. To this task he devoted two hours before breakfast. Plantation affairs occupied him after breakfast until twelve o'clock. To his guests from London, whom he first met at luncheon at one o'clock, he devoted himself until two. From two to four he spent in his library alone. At 4.15 to the minute he waited the appearance of the family and household in the drawing-room. At 4.35 Bulala at the door announced, "Dinner is ready, sir." The dinner here was served in courses, sherry or Madeira was handed, and champagne served on special occasions. Never claret or French wines. The cook, Abraham Fire-All, had been trained by the great Cupidon at Cannon's Point, and as Mrs. Couper devoted most of her time to the supervision of the

housekeeping, the table was an excellent one. A
great point was made of the desserts. By 5.30 the
cloth was drawn, when the ladies went to the drawing-room. Cigars were placed before the men,
Mr. Couper filled his second glass of wine, wished
"Good fortune and health" to all, and retired to his
study. The men smoked, drank one or two glasses
of sherry, and joined the ladies. No whiskey or
brandy was ever served at meals, but they were
placed on the sideboard for the convenience of the
gentlemen guests.

The English visitors left after three days, when,
presumably, the young people breathed sighs of relief and proceeded to have a delightful time. It
was on this occasion that a great boat race took
place at Broughton Island, the home of Mr. Thomas
Forman.

Up to the time of the Civil War, James Hamilton
Couper's life had been eminently successful and
satisfactory. He had executed perfectly every
trust committed to his charge. He was the leading agriculturist of the South, and occupied a position of honor in his community and state. He
had retired to a delightful and comfortable home
at Altama, with a sweet and gentle wife, and
daughters and sons who were gifted and attractive and above all *good*. His means were sufficient

and his prospects promising, and he might well look forward to a happy old age, as a reward for his diligence, unselfishness, and superior intelligence.

XIII

THE HALCYON DAYS

WITH the advent of the third generation St. Simon's reached perhaps its pleasantest days. Although there was no great wealth, there existed a happier condition. No one was without an easy competence, and many possessed incomes far above the average. The mode of life was simple, but the hospitality was immense, and in some houses the procession of incoming and outgoing guests was continuous. It is no wonder that the Southern housekeeper had to have such large services of china, with at least five sizes of meat platters, and vegetable dishes large enough for soup tureens.

In the summer many planters living along the coast came with their families to enjoy the cool breezes of the ocean, either as visitors or as the owners of cottages, and added by their presence to the pleasures of the resident society.

It was mid-century, and the older generation was passing away. In 1850, Mr. John Couper, father of James Hamilton Couper, left "this best of all possible worlds" at the age of ninety-one. The only portraits left of his wife and himself were painted by a house painter, who on one occasion painted the house at Cannon's Point. He is represented as a very plain old gentleman with a shaven face and strong features, and the complexions of both his wife and himself are a brick-dust red. This was probably the only color the house painter had.

Mrs. Thomas Spalding had died in 1843, and for eight years after her death Mr. Spalding lived alone in the great house on Sapelo. His children and grandchildren made periodic visits, and guests from Savannah and other cities were not infrequent. But books were his chief companions. His manner of life remained unchanged; the same large retinue of servants was retained, and his meals were served ceremoniously, three servants waiting on the lonely old man, as when, in earlier days, fifteen to twenty were seated at the table.

If it was any consolation to him, he could feel that his life had been absolutely successful. He had been happily married, his children were comfortably settled, he had been just and humane to the human beings committed to his charge, and he had lived for forty-nine years in the home that he hoped would be the seat of the Spalding family.

He had been eminent in public life and successful
financially, almost the whole of Sapelo being now
in his possession, and he might well say, as he did,
at the end of a noble life, "Sapelo, c' est moi!"

In January 1851, Thomas Spalding died at the
age of seventy-seven, leaving his entire property
to a child of four, his grandson, Thomas Spalding.
This boy, a sister, and a younger brother, Bourke,
were the only descendants in the male line.

Charles Spalding Wylly was fifteen at the time
of his grandfather's death.   He had been sent before he was twelve to the famous school of Coates
and Searle in Charleston, and remained five years
in this admirable place of instruction.   There were
twenty-five boarders and sixty day scholars.
Charles Wylly from Georgia and the two Toutants
of Louisiana being the only "foreigners" since they
came from barbarian communities, in the estima-
tions of Charlestonians.   Many of his schoolmates
became noted in later life, and a number gave their
lives for the Lost Cause.

In 1853, Charles was sent to the military school
at Marietta, Georgia, where his Georgia acquaint-
anceship was enlarged.   The cadet battalion numbered 160 to 185, and the first class to graduate had
every member killed in battle by 1863.

The military institution could not be called ideal,

but the *esprit* was high, and had not the disaster of war destroyed the buildings and dissipated the funds it is possible that the G. M. I. might have become a valuable state institution. As early as 1822 Governor Troup had said in his message to the legislature, "Prepare now for the last and coming resort, by the establishment in every state of military schools, foundries, armories, arsenals and powder manufactories." The school was not established until 1850, the arsenals and factories not at all.

January 1856 found Charles Wylly at home, just entering his twentieth year, in perfect vigor of mind and body. He had not graduated, owing to a foolish *emeute,* nearly approaching a mutiny, of the senior class of which he was a member.

He was well prepared for the choice of a profession, and in any but a Southern state he would have chosen one. But however high the aspiration, however studious the habits, the return to the environment of a Southern plantation was, for a young man, usually fatal to ambition. Surrounded by servants, with horses, dogs, guns, and boats at his command, there seemed to be no higher aim than to drive dull care away, and outdoor sports were the daily task and pleasure of most of the Southern boys.

For forty miles around every house was open to Charles Wylly, and many were the homes of relatives. On Sapelo lived his grandfather, uncles, and aunts. At Hopeton were his first cousins. On the coast he visited the Grants at Elizafield, the Troups at Broadfield, and the Dents at Hofwyl. On St. Simon's he was oftenest at Cannon's Point and Retreat, though he also visited his widowed grandmother Wylly at the Village.

"In her old age, at seventy," he writes, "I remember thinking her the most stately and lovely woman I had ever seen. After her husband's death she never changed the fashion of her dress. Tall and erect, she always wore a black silk gown, with a kerchief of the snowiest cambric crossed over her breast. Her snow white hair of great length and thickness was coiled around a beautifully shaped head, and surmounted by a cap with wide lapels. She was dignity itself, exacting from all, even her sons and daughters, the most scrupulous respect. To her grandchildren she was more generous than her means warranted, tipping them in English fashion. When visited by the young ones, she would lead them into the drawing-room, where portraits of Nelson and Wellington hung, and bid them mark the appearance of 'the greatest men of the nineteenth century.'"

In truth she never became an American, and looked with no favor on those who had brought about the independence of the United States.

To the whole island she was "the lady of the manor," and greatly beloved by rich and poor. Her house was large, and often filled with relatives, some coming from the Bahamas and England. Her servants were wonderfully trained, perhaps not to the nicety of Mrs. Brailsford's, whose butler, as the small Charles Wylly was about to help himself to rice, whispered, "with fish, Mass Charles, only potatoes and bread."

After Mrs. Wylly's death in 1850, her three spinster daughters lived on comfortably at the Village, immersed in the cares of house, garden, and poultry yard, and as kind and indulgent to their numerous nieces and nephews as their mother had been. They were keenly interested in people, and one of them would sit for hours on the front piazza, looking through a telescope down the road to the front gate, hoping to catch a glimpse of someone passing on the highway! It is pleasant to know that eventually two of the old ladies moved to Savannah to live, and led quite a gay life, going every summer to New York, where they attended lectures and concerts and even went to the theatre!

Their nearest neighbors to the south were the

Goulds, who lived three miles away. Here Mr. James Gould had built a house which he called Black Banks after the river on which it stood. In 1844, he sold this to his brother Horace, who married Deborah Abbott the following year. The Stevenses and Abbotts had recently come to St. Simon's and settled on the west side of the island below Frederica. This place had been deeded by old Mr. Spalding to his grandson, Thomas Spalding Wylly, Charles Wylly's oldest brother, who sold it in 1854 to Mr. John Stevens for a thousand dollars.

Below Black Banks was Kelvyn Grove, the Cater home. Benjamin Cater had married Miss Armstrong, a cousin of the Wyllys' and the poor young mother had died at the birth of her little daughter, Annie, who was now growing up with the third generation of young people on St. Simon's.

After his father's death, James Hamilton Couper came into Cannon's Point, and also bought the Hamilton estate below Frederica. Cannon's Point was used as a summer home, and here was gathered everything that could attract the young. In the garden almost every known flower bloomed to perfection; in the orchard, figs, peaches, pomegranates, and oranges ripened in profusion; in the stables were numbers of good riding horses; while a river for boating flowed within a stone's cast of the house.

The greatest attraction at Cannon's Point, however, was the master of the house, a man who never said anything that was not well considered, and whose family treasured every word that fell from his lips.

"I recall meeting a visitor who had spent the night at Cannon's Point," Charles Wylly wrote, "and my saying, 'I know you had a pleasant visit.' 'An instructive one,' he answered; 'I was shown to Mr. Couper's library, and our business interview was quickly and satisfactorily concluded. I was told the tide would not allow me to leave, and Mr. Couper hoped I would spend the night. A specimen of coral from the Pacific lying on the table, Mr. Couper took it up, and explained most clearly and elaborately how, by the labor of the tiny insects, islands, almost continents, had been built up in the Eastern oceans. He was most interesting, fortifying his statements with quotations from Sir Charles Lyell and other geologists. Looking over a memorandum, he then said that he was forced to keep an engagement, and adding that dinner would be at 4.30, he excused himself. He had not left five minutes before Mrs. Couper came in, saying that she was sorry that Mr. Couper had been called out, but that he broke an engagement for no one. Seeing the coral, she launched into the same account of the labors of the insect world repeating word for word what I had already heard. She left, saying that dinner would be hurried. Who should enter then but Alexander Couper! He walked straight to the cursed rock, and again I heard Mr. Couper's essay reeled off, word for word. He then said that a hive of bees was about to swarm, and asked if I would like to help him. I decidedly declined, and he then left, saying he would send Robert to me. Robert came, and was already started on the thrice-told tale, when I begged, on account of the heat, the privilege of a littie air. So you see, Charles, my visit was, as I have said, a very instructive but not very entertaining one.' "

Charles Wylly was a frequent visitor at Cannon's Point. He was fond of all of his cousins, and of the oldest, Hamilton, he said, "Take him, all in all, he possessed more natural gifts than any man I ever met. With a mind that imbibed all the beauties of literature and art, and an exquisite sense of humor, he was by far the most interesting man I have ever known."

Alexander, the second son, was always erratic, but fearless and spirited, and fond of hunting and

outdoor life. John displayed real promise as a
landscape painter. James was genial, full of
humor, and the life of the house. Robert, the
youngest son, was a scholar, as interested in science
as in the classics, with a gift for drawing. The
oldest of the daughters, Margaret, was lovely in
person and character, and the youngest, Rebecca
Isabel, witty and delightful.

Mr. Couper planned careers for all of his sons.
Hamilton was to be a lawyer; Aleck, a merchant;
John, an artist, and so on. Only two fulfilled their
destiny. Hamilton was educated at Yale, studied
law at Harvard, and practised at first in the law of-
fice of his father's friend, Mr. John Lord of New
York. But his heart was in the South, and he returned to settle in Savannah, where he became
United States District Attorney. John went to
college in Athens, Georgia, and then to Philadelphia to study art. He had not finished his course
when the war ended it.

Mention has already been made of the boat racing. It was one of the favorite sports of the coast
planters, and almost every plantation had its racing
boats and a crew of trained oarsmen. Mr. Couper
had an especial talent for boat building, and always
designed his own, having them made on the place

under his supervision. The two most famous of the Couper boats were the *Walk-Away* and the *Becky Sharp,* the latter a dugout, made of a single cypress log. Mr. Couper also trained his oarsmen himself, entering his boats in many races at home, and in the regattas held in Savannah and Charleston.

The *Becky Sharp* won a memorable race in Charleston, an account of which Mr. Couper wrote to his son Hamilton, who was at that time in New York.

CHARLESTON, 20*th November,* 1852.

MY DEAR HAMILTON:

I telegraphed you at 5 oc, on the 17th instant, mentioning the victory of the *Becky Sharp,* and sent you the *Charleston Mercury,* containing an account of the race. The *Becky Sharp* was the admired of all admirers, and her fame is spread far and wide. And she deserves her reputation.

There was a heavy swell, a strong wind, and a current of 2 miles against her, and yet she made the distance of a mile, less 12 yards, in 6 minutes, without pressing her crew. She rode the waves like a duck, skimming from wave to wave, with a continuous gliding motion. Her crew of 8 oars consisted of Jesse, Sandy, Malbrouck, Isaac and Quash (Dr. Screven's), Edward and Charles (Mr. Forman's), and Carolina (Mr. R. Spalding's) —

and a finer one never rowed. They kept time perfectly, were perfectly cool, and not a false stroke was made. It was a pleasure to sit behind them — I steered myself. Mr. Bourke came on for that purpose, but was so *tight,* that I found it necessary to be my own coxswain. In 100 yards I perceived that the race was mine, and after that distance my only competitor was the *North State,* a very keen clinker built boat from North Carolina, of 10 oars, manned by a pilot from Cape Fear River, the pick of 50. She was soon, however, shaken off, and was left four open lengths in the rear, with so little effort that they threw up their hands and cheered repeatedly; and on rounding the coming-out boat, they struck up Jesse's favorite song of "Slippers, Shoes and White Stockings."

The distance might have been increased to 6 or 7 instead of 5 lengths.

The entries were,

The Unknown					
(South Carolina)	44	feet long.		16	oars.
Wrecker's Daughter					
(North Carolina)	"	"	"	14	"
North State					
(North Carolina)	45	"	"	10	"
W. W. Woodworth					
(New York)	36	"	"	6	"
New York					
(New York)	38	"	"	4	"
A Carolina boat				12	"

There were 8 boats in the second race and 10 in the third.

On Thursday the Regatta Club gave a capital dinner. I was placed at the right of the president, and the first toast was, "James Hamilton Couper and the *Becky Sharp*," with 8 cheers. The attention I have received is unbounded. To-day I have dined with Governor Bennet—tomorrow with the Carolina Institute.

John, James and Robert enjoy themselves highly, having made many acquaintances. They have been to four plays, and are every day seeing interesting objects. We leave for home on the 22nd. The whole regatta has been a brilliant affair, and I doubt whether so many fine boats were ever before brought together, certainly never in America.

Very affectionately, dear Hamilton, yours,

J. HAMILTON COUPER.

Mr. Thomas Forman of Broughton Island was as much interested in boat racing as Mr. Couper, and Charles Wylly was present at a famous race which took place in the late fifties. The three boats entered belonged to Mr. Forman, Mr. Couper, and Mr. Randolph Spalding. The loser was to pay for the wine for the feast following the race. Each owner steered his own boat, and Mr. Couper won in his *Sunny South*. Mr. Spalding's boat came in second, and Mr. Forman's last. So Mr.

Forman paid for the wine as well as for the bounteous feast, which was served on a flatboat tied to the landing.

Next to Cannon's Point, the home on St. Simon's that Charles Wylly visited most frequently was Retreat. Mallory Page King, the third son of the family, was his college mate and particular chum, and they had the same tastes, both being fonder of social and outdoor life than of work or study. "Both of us had eaten too freely of the fruit of the Land of the Lotus," Charles Wylly admits.

Mr. King, having entered public life, was away from home most of the time. After the Mexican War he was sent by the government to California, to examine the newly acquired territory, and in 1850 he returned to that state as first Collector of the Port of San Francisco, and aided in establishing law and order in that wild community. In his efforts on behalf of a Panama Canal he was ahead of his time, and he was the first to advocate building a transcontinental railway from Brunswick, Georgia, to San Diego, California.

As her husband was away from home so much of the time, Mrs. King took entire charge of the estate, supervising everything from the planting to the shipping and marketing of the crops. She

was considered the most successful agriculturist
on the island, being noted for her careful selection
of seed, through which the improvement of her cotton staple was assured. The whole estate —
fields, gardens, orchards, poultry yards, dairy, and
Negro quarters — was pervaded with a sense of
teeming fruitfulness and solid comfort. Mrs.
King attended to the feeding and clothing of the
hundreds of slaves belonging to her, and was a
just and kind mistress, always ready to listen to and
sympathize with them, supervising their religious
training, and visiting them when they were sick.
In addition to being a fine business woman, she was
a charming hostess, and made her home delightful
for husband, children, and friends.

By the end of the fifties Thomas Butler King,
the oldest son of the family, grown to manhood, was
able to help his mother with the management of
Retreat, and so well was this done that its brand on
a bale of cotton ensured fifty cents a pound, whilst
elsewhere forty-four cents was the best price ob-
tainable.

The surroundings of Retreat were most attractive. A superb avenue of live oaks, which had
been planted by James Spalding in 1750, led to the
front gate. To reach the house one passed through
a lovely garden. The plan for this was designed

by William Audley Couper, who had married Hannah Lord King, the oldest daughter of the family. In the centre of the garden was a large star, surrounded by an octagon, enclosed in a square. Paths led from every point of the star out to the broad path enclosing the whole. Mrs. King would have no flower in her garden that was odorless. "Plants without souls," she called them, so no camellias flaunted their waxen beauty; but roses, violets, heliotrope, and sweet olio were there in glorious profusion. In a letter written to one of her sons at Yale, Mrs. King says, "I wish you could see the garden this morning. I counted 96 different varieties of roses in bloom, besides other flowers."

The arboretum at Retreat was one of the finest in the country at this time; plants, shrubs, and trees from many lands grew there to perfection, Mr. King having brought many of these back from California.

There were five sons and four daughters in the King family, and at this time the house was one of joyousness. It was a veritable Liberty Hall, where everyone, old or young, did as he pleased, and chose what he liked in the way of amusement. The entertaining of visitors was frequent, for though the house was not large, an annex gave room enough and to spare. The young people danced at night to the music of the plantation violin, sang, played games, or improvised theatricals.

Sarah Butler, the daughter of Fanny Kemble and Pierce Butler, who had been the little "Ruling Lady" of Butler's Island, gives an account of these festivities in notes written to Margaret Couper and Georgia King. Her father had brought her down to St. Simon's as a young lady in the fifties, and she writes from Hampton Point.

Sunday afternoon, *June 10th.*
My dear Maggie:

The glimpse I had of you to-day was so fleeting, that I forgot to ask you something which I intended to propose.

Father is going up to Butler's Island tomorrow to remain there, sleeping at The Thicket, until Tuesday afternoon, so availing myself of your kindness and Georgia King's, I am going down to The Retreat to spend the day and night, taking the liberty of keeping your horse and buggy for the purpose, unless so doing will inconvenience you.

But I want to propose something that will make it much pleasanter — for me — and ensure me a warmer welcome, and that is that you will go with me. I have made up my mind about it, so just add this favor to the long list which you and your parents have already conferred — the last which you can grant, since we leave for the North next Saturday.

Pray don't meet this request by a refusal, or an offer to drive down in your double carriage; that will not be half as pleasant as driving down independently by ourselves, with a little "tiger" behind the buggy to open the gates for us; so come over early enough to admit of our starting about 10 o'clock, and reaching our destination before the extreme heat of the day. You told me you had nothing smaller than the hat-box which you took down on our former visit. Bring over your nightcap, tooth brush, etc, in a package, and I will give you half of the little valise which I used on the same occasion.

Remember me most kindly to your father and mother, and believe me

Yours affectionately
SARAH BUTLER.

By the way did you enjoy the consolations of religion after your drive to-day?

It was a twelve-mile drive from Hampton Point down to Retreat. A beautiful drive along the old highway, under the overarching trees, and the two young girls must have enjoyed it thoroughly, with all they had to talk about and the pr spect of an enchanting visit at the end.

Many years later, Sarah, who was then Mrs.
Wister of Philadelphia, wrote to Georgia King.

Georgy, do you recollect the little party and the
private theatricals? And Julia Van Renselaer, so
handsome and elegant, accomplished and agreeable,
and selfish and snobbish and spoiled? And Virginia, so clever and piquante, and looking so well in
her prince-page's dress. And Lord, and Butler.
. . . And your friend, Mrs. Troup, and her
pretty, graceful sisters; and Mr. Postell, and his
pigeon-wing in the quadrille! And you as the
dowager duenna. . . . I remember my sunrise
ride with Lord next morning, and the Demere's
magnolia tree deep in the woods. . . . It's like
yesterday to me.

Your affectionate old friend,

S. B. W.

Retreat was now at its most prosperous and happiest period. The daughters won all hearts by
their grace and courtesy, and to the third —
Georgia — had been granted every gift of attraction. Inheriting the lovely voice of her mother
and her grandfather Page, she sang so beautifully
that even middle-aged gentlemen took the long
row across the sound to have the pleasure of hearing her. She played the organ in the little island church, and led the choir, and Charles Wylly

remembered seeing the melodeon arrive, perched in the rear of the conveyance, on the front seat of which sat Butler and Georgia King. "And then," he says, "we had singing that would draw the angels from heaven."

The King sons were educated by tutors who prepared them for college, and Georgia, who was a fine student, shared their studies. Many years later, a niece, who was a college graduate, said to her, "Your generation, Aunt Georgia, may have been cultivated, but it was not educated." To which her aunt quietly replied, "At least, my dear, we knew how to *spell*."

The impression made on Audubon will give some idea of the Kings' delightful island home. The great ornithologist was on his way to St. Augustine, in the schooner *Agnes,* when he was compelled, because of a storm, to put in at the south end of St. Simon's. "I made for the shore," he wrote, "met a gentleman, Mr. King, on the beach, presented him my card, and was immediately invited to dinner. I visited his garden, got into such agreeable conversation and quarters, that I was fain to think I had landed on some one of those fairy islands said to have existed in the Golden Age."

The decade preceding the Civil War was indeed the Golden Age of St. Simon's.

XIV

THE END

"When the year 1860 drew to a close," Charles Wylly wrote, "1861, big with momentous issues of coming events, cast its shadow upon a people absolutely ignorant and heedless of the gravity of the situation. I say ignorant in the sense of being, as a mass, totally unaware of the immense superiority in numbers and resources of the states which opposed them, and ignorant of the fact that it takes years of careful preparation to gather the material with which to wage a successful war. In lieu of arms, the Southerners had confidence in their own marksmanship, tried and proved in woodland sports. In the place of numbers, they had an unfounded belief that each Southern soldier would equal a platoon of Northern invaders. Skillfully led up to the fever point of secession by two superbly gifted orators, who, with tongues of fire, declared in every district of the state there would be a bloodless revolution, Georgia, on January 19, 1861, declared herself freed from the Union.

"With 1861 came four years of matchless endeavor to create a nation, and to give to the world a new republic and a new flag, one with the stripes erased, but with the stars still shining. If ever faith manifested itself it was during those years, when deep-rooted convictions of guaranteed constitutional rights were arrayed in hopeless conflict against the spirit of the age, and the awakened conscience of mankind."

Charles Wylly had finally selected the profession of civil engineering, and in 1857 went West with an engineering corps to lay out a route for the Southern Pacific Railway. He was in northern Louisiana when that state seceded from the Union, and the governor called on Tensas Parish to enlist one hundred men for a period of three years. Eighty young men offered their services on the first day at what is now Tallulah, the county seat, and elected George Waddell of Lake Providence as captain, and Charles Wylly first sergeant of their company.

Ordered immediately to Virginia, their three days' journey was a triumphant tour. At every station they were met by delegations of ladies bearing flags and flowers, and offering collations to "our gallant boys." At Vicksburg, a Miss Arnold, draped in the state's colors, recited "Aux Armes"

CHARLES SPALDING WYLLY
(A Photograph Taken in 1905)

to the company lined up to board the cars. She was very handsome and, had not the call "All aboard!" been shouted, would have received a half-dozen offers in as many minutes, and some of them most desirable ones. Convinced that the war would be over in a year at most, these enthusiastic young men reached Virginia, and were enrolled in the 4th Louisiana Battalion.

And then began the days that tried the souls of men and women. The world has never known greater heroism than that of the men of the South. Coming, many of them, from homes of luxury, they endured unflinchingly four years of bitter warfare until, reduced to starvation, barefooted, and clothed in rags, they were finally forced to yield to an overwhelming force.

In December 1861, a booming of cannon was heard to the northward of St. Simon's, and soon after word was received that Port Royal had been abandoned. The evacuation of St. Simon's was ordered, and the women, who were alone in their homes, hurriedly packed what was absolutely necessary, buried their silver, and closed their houses. The three old maids at the Village instructed their trusted head man to bury their silver under the potato patch, and left for Darien. When no silver was found after the war, the old Negro protested that he had never told a soul of its whereabouts. Nor had he, but when he had told his son to plant potatoes the following year, he had added the words, *"Dig deep!"*

St. Simon's shared the fate of the conquered South. It was occupied by the Federals; many of the homes were burned, and horses were stabled in the little church. Fields were abandoned, fences torn down for firewood, and gardens and lawns trampled by straying stock. In spite of the universal destruction, the garden at Retreat remained beautiful enough to impress even an enemy, for the historian Thomas Higginson wrote of it, "The loveliest garden I have ever seen, and filled with hyacinthine odors."

Sorrow had come to Retreat just before the war, for in 1859 the oldest son had died, followed in six months' time by the splendid mother. Mr. King, although a Northerner, had been among the foremost in the long fight for Southern rights which anticipated the War of Secession. On the threatening of that war, he had been sent by Governor Brown to Europe, as Commissioner from the State of Georgia, and he advised sending cotton to England to establish a gold credit for the South. Unfortunately his wise advice was not followed, but he did not live to see the ruin of the land of his adoption, for he died before the war was over.

His four remaining sons all went to war, Henry Lord King accompanied by his body servant, Neptune Small. At the battle of Fredericksburg, volunteers were called for to carry dispatches through a dangerous section. Lord King volunteered for the duty, and went to his death as coolly and gracefully as though entering a drawing-room. He accomplished his mission, but was killed on his return, his body being pierced by seventeen bullets. None of his comrades would dare the shower of shot and shell, but Neptune brought his body out and carried it home, and he lies to-day in the little churchyard at Frederica.

Neptune was told that he could stay at home, but he preferred to join young Cuyler King at the front, and was allowed to go. Once when they were encamped in the mountains of Virginia, the two were lying on a hillside when the full moon rose. "High water on de bar, Mass Tip," said Neptune. He was looking beyond the mountains of Virginia, and seeing his beautiful island home, with the full moon rising over the Atlantic.

The three remaining brothers, Mallory, Floyd, and Cuyler, fought gallantly through the whole war, and though in more than a hundred engagements, were none of them wounded. They lived to meet the harder fate of those who survived.

When the war was over, the young men who had left the Georgia coast in such high spirits returned to find a ravaged and ruined land. The scourge, which had been predicted by their ancestors of New Inverness, had come. An entire people had been reduced to poverty, for the whole system of industry had been based on the permanence in value of slave holdings. Fields that until then had yielded immense returns lay idle, reverting to swamp and forest, while the freed slaves reveled in sloth, or supported themselves by chance employment or petty thieving. By the act of a madman the South was delivered over to the horrors of Reconstruction, and the magnanimity shown in the terms of surrender by Grant, and approved by Lincoln, was dissipated in the fierce heat of party hatred. The crime of the Fourteenth and Fifteenth Amendments was perpetrated.

Charles Wylly was typical of the gentlemen of the South, who fought through four years of heartbreaking hardships, were conquered, and returned to find their homes in ruins and their wealth gone; and who, facing the situation without a murmur, turned to any work their hands could find, and strove to gather together the fragments of a lost prosperity.

Only occasionally did these brave hearts sink into cynicism and despair. A planter on Back River, having spent his all from day to day, disappeared, leaving on his table three packets, each containing a little gold. On these were written: "This for my last week's board"; "This for my funeral expenses"; "This for Masses for my soul." On the last was added, "Go to Wharf No. 3. On its cap-sill you will find a rope. Pull on the rope, and you will find me." *Requiescat in pace!*

The fate of one family on the Georgia coast was typical of all.

James Hamilton Couper never approved of the war. While he believed in the constitutional right of secession, he recognized its futility. His five sons went into the war. Hamilton volunteered in 1861, was Captain of the Oglethorpe Light Infantry, and died in Virginia of typhoid fever on October 20 of the same year. John, who had always been delicate, enlisted, to his mother's despair, and died the following year of enteric fever in a lonely Virginia farmhouse. Aleck would only enlist as a private, fought gallantly throughout the war, and returned to spend the rest of his life as a hermit in the deep woods of Altama. James, who had married Eudora Harper of Vicksburg, was a dashing soldier, and distinguished himself at the siege of Vicksburg by floating at night down the river, past the Federal fleet, to carry dispatches beyond the lines. Robert, entering the war at seventeen from the University of Virginia, refused to leave his cousin John Fraser when the latter was mortally wounded, and was captured by the enemy and imprisoned on Johnson's Island, never recovering entirely from the hardships endured during those years.

In 1860, Margaret Couper had married Robert Mackay Stiles and gone to live in Savannah, so only Mr. and Mrs. Couper and their daughter Rebecca were living at Altama at this time. Three years before the war, at the age of sixty-three, Mr. Couper had burdened himself with a debt of more than $80,000. Had the Civil War not ensued, all would probably have gone well; but with a lien on land and Negroes, and with the Negroes freed, all of Hopeton, Altama, and Carrs' Island was taken for debt by Richard Corbin of Paris, from whose two daughters Mr. Couper had bought the land. To the credit of young Richard Corbin it should be mentioned that he ran away from home, came to America, and fought gallantly for the Confederacy.

The death of his two most promising sons was a blow from which Mr. Couper never recovered, and he lived to see the entire work of his lifetime in ruins. In 1863, he suffered a paralytic stroke, and in 1866 he died.

Fannie Butler, who had come down to St. Simon's that year, with her father, Pierce Butler, gives in her Southern book a pathetic account of his funeral.

HAMPTON POINT, *July 9th,* 1866.

DEAREST SARAH:

Mr. James Hamilton Couper died last week, and was buried at the little church here on the island yesterday. The whole thing was sad in the extreme, and a fit illustration of his people and country. Three years ago he was smitten with paralysis, the result of grief at the loss of his sons, loss of his property, and the ruin of all his hopes and prospects; since which his life has been one of great suffering, until a few days ago, when death released him.

Hearing from his son James of his death, and the time fixed for his funeral, my father and I drove down in the old mule cart, our only conveyance, nine miles to the church. Here a most terrible scene of desolation met us. The steps of the church were broken down, so we had to walk up a plank to get in; the roof was fallen in so that the sun streamed down on our heads; while the seats were all cut up and marked with the names of the Northern soldiers who had been quartered there during the war. The graveyard was so overgrown with weeds and bushes, and tangled with web-like grey moss, that we had difficulty in making our way through to the freshly dug grave.

In about half an hour the funeral party arrived. The coffin was in a cart drawn by one miserable horse, and was followed by the Couper family on foot, having come this way from the landing, one mile off. From the cart to the grave the coffin was carried by four old family Negroes, faithful to the end. Standing there I said to myself, "Some day justice will be done, and the Truth shall be heard above the political din of slander and lies, and the Northern people shall see things as they are, and not through the dark veil of envy, hatred and malice."

Fannie Butler realized that the Southerners were utterly crushed, and with her warm and generous heart she felt deeply for them. Her father had shown his sympathy during the war by visiting the prison camps at the North and doing all that he could for the Southern prisoners.

Another staunch friend was Mr. John Lord of New York, who after the war lent young Robert Couper $10,000 to plant with, saying that if he made a failure of the undertaking, he could consider it a gift. Like all other attempts at planting on the Georgia coast, it was a failure under the changed conditions.

Even Mr. Butler, with ample means at his command, was not able to make a success of it. By 1866, his slaves, though freed, had all returned to Butler's Island. Even those who had been sold three years before the war returned, and seven worked their way back from the upcountry. And these were the slaves who had suffered the tortures of Dante's *Inferno* under their Butler masters!

When Pierce Butler and his daughter went up to the island, nearly four hundred Negroes came to the house to shake their hands, saying, "Tank de Lord, Missus, we 's back, and sees you and Massa again!" When told they were free and their own masters, they cried, "No, Missus. We b'long to you. We be yours as long as we lib."

One old Negro had guarded the property in his care so well from Northern marauders that he had ninety sheep and thirty cows to return to Mr. Butler. An old couple came up from St. Simon's with five dollars in silver half dollars tied up in a bag, which they said a Yankee captain had given them the second year of the war for some chickens. This money the two old people had kept through three years of want and suffering, because it had been paid for fowls belonging to their master.

Mr. Butler was greatly touched by this act of faithfulness and gave the old couple the same amount in bills, intending to keep the silver and have something made of it to commemorate the act.

It was in this year that Morris, the grandson of Major Butler's head man Morris, died. Pierce Butler writes of this event, "It is with very sad feelings that I write to tell you of the death of Morris, the head man of General's Island. He was attacked with fever, and died in four days. Dr. R. attended him, and I nursed him, but his disease was malignant in its character, and the medicine produced no effect. To me the loss is irreparable. He was by far the most intelligent Negro I have ever known among our slaves. His sense and judgment were those of the white race, rather than the black, and the view he took of the present position of his race was sensible and correct. He knew that freedom entailed self-dependence and labor, not idleness, and he set an example to those whose labors he directed by never sparing himself where work was to be done."

Unfortunately the example of this fine colored man had little effect on the Butler Negroes. Mr.

Butler died the next year, and until 1870 his daughter Fannie continued to manage their Georgia plantations. She found it almost impossible to make the Negroes work, as these were the trying days of Reconstruction, when everything possible was done by the Northern carpetbaggers to turn the Negroes against the Southern whites.

In 1870, Fannie Butler married the Reverend James W. Leigh of England, the second son of Lord Leigh. Her husband was deeply interested in religious work among the Negroes, and they returned for several winters to the South. Finding at last that their efforts were of no avail, they relinquished the attempt, and their plantations were turned over to managers, and in the end abandoned as unprofitable.

At the beginning of the war all of the Spaldings had left Sapelo, because of the Federal gunboats in the sound, and it was taken possession of by runaway Negroes. These were dislodged with some difficulty when the family finally returned. In 1870, Thomas Spalding, "the child of four," attained his majority and took possession of what had been his grandfather's princely legacy. The slaves had been freed, the great house was a ruin, the land only an asset. Thousands of acres of pine lands had been sold for taxes, titles had been lost, and the land, in many cases, was not even claimed. Thomas and Bourke Spalding, with their brother-in-law, A. C. McKinley, now moved to Sapelo, and in spite of the ruin wrought by war, the island was to them still beautiful and dear. Life was happy, as it always is to the young, and one of them could write, "Will any people ever live on Sapelo who will love it as did those three families?"

The end of the Spalding library was typical of the end of most of those in the South. After the war Charles Wylly tried to pursue his profession of civil engineering, but finding this unprofitable, he turned to the lumber industry, now beginning to be an important one in Darien. He married a Miss Whittaker of Florida, and had a dearly loved daughter, but in a few years lost both wife and child. It was of these days that he wrote, "In the sad years from 1868 to 1878, Mr. Spalding's carefully selected library saved me, I think, from mental, possibly bodily death. Often when the five o'clock whistle called me to welcome work, I have laid aside the book that for a time had drawn a veil over what was. In the end the Spalding library came into the possession of my brother William, who had married the widow of Thomas Spalding. After her death he sent it to New York for sale. There it fell among thieves, and returned minus its most valuable works. In 1894 the remaining books were sold, I should think, by the pound, and utterly scattered." The only work that came into Charles Wylly's possession was an edition of Rousseau in thirty-nine volumes, calf bound, which was published in Paris in 1792. On the flyleaf of the first volume is written, "Marquis de Montalet, 1792. Thomas Spalding, 1813. Charles Spalding, 1835. Charles Spalding Wylly, 1886."

After the war but few of the old families returned to live on St. Simon's. Retreat had been presented to the Negroes by the Federal soldiers, but was finally restored to the Kings, when it became the home of Colonel Mallory King and his family. The three daughters had married and gone to live in Savannah, Florence becoming the wife of General Henry R. Jackson, Georgia of Mr. Joseph J. Wilder, and Virginia of Mr. John Nesbit.

The Goulds were still at Black Banks, and Annie Cater, having married Mr. John Postell, was in her old home, Kelvyn Grove. The Stevenses and Abbotts were on the west side of the island, but everyone else had moved away, most of them going to Brunswick, which had now superseded Darien as a place of business.

James Maxwell Couper, who had taken charge of his father's estate, sold Cannon's Point to Mr. Shadman, whose son William married Emma, the second of the Postell daughters. The young couple lived at Cannon's Point until the house was burned, when they moved to the south end of the island, where Mrs. Shadman and her younger sister Annie Postell still live.

In 1897, Charles Wylly wrote of Cannon's Point, "Around the blackened walls of this house, even now topped with its green crown of date and palm, cling no memories but those of love and courtesy, intermixt with a personal individuality, charming to remember. A trinity of the good, the beautiful and the true."

The Hamilton estate was sold by James Couper in 1874 to the Dodge-Meigs Company, who, with their successors, the Hilton and Dodge Lumber Company, operated a sawmill there until 1886. The name of the place was changed to St. Simon's Mills, and it was here that the timber for the Brooklyn Bridge was sawed.

The dwelling house and all the outhouses of the Village had been burned, and the cedar grove bordering the creek had been felled by a pencil manufacturer. The last of the Couper holdings on St. Simon's was Long Island, and this was sold

Courtesy of T. Morrison Carnegie

THE RUINS OF DUNGENESS

in 1895 to a company which planned the erection of a hotel on the beach. Not a foot of all the land acquired by such industry remained in the family, and almost every cent received from these sales was lost in a futile attempt to continue rice planting. And yet James Couper could write in 1912: —

Whilst belonging to the class of slave owners, and a Confederate soldier, I say, without hesitation, that no greater benefit ever befell any country than the emancipation of the Negroes in the South. The Anglo-Saxon then found that, with his own brain and muscle, he could make the lands of the South the garden spot of the earth.

It is true that a civilized people should have found another solution for the removal of slavery, besides war, but the Fire-Eaters of the South and the Abolitionists of the North, the latter aided by such women as Mrs. Stowe and Fanny Kemble, women of marked talent, are responsible for the misery and suffering incurred in its solution. Slavery was forced upon us by England, and the slaves were brought from Africa and sold to us by New Englanders. Let the world be fair, and it will be seen that all the blame does not rest upon the shoulders of the South.

Thank God, it is over, and I have had the privilege of seeing my people emerge from the dark days of Reconstruction to the present with its glorious promise.

In 1874, Sidney Lanier came to Brunswick to visit his brother-in-law, Mr. Henry Day, and in 1875 he wrote "The Marshes of Glynn." The great oak is still standing on the edge of the marsh near Brunswick, beneath which he is said to have written this exquisite poem. Mr. and Mrs. James Couper were living in Brunswick at this time, and it was at their house that Sidney Lanier first read this poem aloud from the original manuscript. Inspired by the beauty of the Georgia coast, he also wrote, "A Marsh Song," "A Marsh Hymn," "Between Dawn and Sunrise," and the glorious "Sunrise," which was written just before his death in Baltimore in 1881.

The first post-war benefactor of St. Simon's was the Reverend Anson G. P. Dodge, who came to Christ Church as the Episcopal minister in 1884. Finding the old church in a ruinous condition, he built the present one on its foundations. His young wife dying in India, her body was brought back to St. Simon's and buried in the little churchyard, beneath the old oaks and the long gray moss which she had found so melancholy. After several years, Mr. Dodge married Miss Anna Gould of Black Banks. Their only child died in infancy, and as a memorial to his son Mr. Dodge erected the Anson Dodge orphanage, which stands on the site of the old land port of Frederica.

Mr. Dodge's was a consecrated life, and he was a blessing to St. Simon's in its darkest days. In love for God and his fellow man he forgot himself, and merged his own life in that of the destitute and fatherless. He himself lies in the little graveyard now, where so many other noble dead are buried.

In 1882, Captain Charles Wylly married his cousin, Rebecca Isabel Couper, and later on they moved from Darien to Brunswick to be with her mother, who lived to the age of eighty-seven. It was about this time that Charles Wylly had charge of the sale of Altama. After the war Mr. Corbin and his son Richard had made Altama their winter home, and attempted to continue rice planting on Hopeton. The old gentleman spent most of his time raking the long gray moss, which he detested, from the great oaks surrounding the house, but making a failure of both attempts, father and son returned to Paris. Hopeton and Altama were offered for sale, and bought by a set of Quakers from Ohio. They also made a failure of planting, and both places were eventually bought by Mr. William Du Pont for a winter home.

Only twice in forty years did Charles Wylly

visit Sapelo, which he had loved so in his youth.
The first time, as he stood at the South End, all
that met his eye was crumbling walls that threatened soon to turn to dust, and the shadows cast by
the great trees surrounding it were no darker than
his thoughts. In this druid-like grove his grandfather, Thomas Spalding, had thought to found in
perpetuity the seat of a family. In the deep mono-
tone of a stormy sea he heard in each incoming wave
the words "To be," followed by "To have," as the
wave broke on the shore, whilst every outgoing
sweep of the surge seemed to sigh, "And nothing
more."

In 1914, Charles Wylly visited Sapelo for the
last time, and found the noble house rebuilt and
standing white and spotless in its beautiful garni-
ture of green. Facing the ocean, it greets the rising sun in its splendor, and bids it farewell as it
sinks to repose. "And the roof covers one," he
writes, "who is not unmindful of what has been,
and not forgetful of the past — Mr. Howard Coffin of Detroit."

It was many years after the war before the pressure of poverty began to be lightened in the South
and the coast people could consider the possibility
of pleasure again. Gradually use began to be made
of the fine beach on St. Simon's, a hotel was built,
and the island became popular as a summer resort.

Jekyl Island was the first to experience the return of prosperity, for in 1886 it was bought from the Du Bignon family by a set of wealthy Northerners, who found it an ideal site for an exclusive club.

In 1924, a causeway was built connecting St. Simon's with the mainland, and reaching the island at Gascoigne's Bluff. In the years that have followed, owing to the munificence of Mr. Howard Coffin, the island has been transformed. On Long Island, which is now called Sea Island, the beautiful Cloister Hotel has been erected. A fine club house stands on the spot where the old King house was burned twenty years ago. A casino, swimming pool, and yacht club add to the pleasure of visitors, and fine golf links and beautiful roadways make St. Simon's one of the most delightful resorts of the South.

Charles Wylly outlived almost his entire generation, the wife whom he so dearly loved having died in 1912. It was during the lonely years following that he wrote his *Memories* and *Annals*, from which most of the foregoing has been taken.

The last but one of his large family, he was left old, lonely, and in straitened circumstances, the sole support he could count on being his small Confederate pension. And yet, in spite of the utterly changed conditions of his life, — and, to one of his warm-heartedness and lavish generosity, not being able to *give* was one of the hardest things he had to bear, — he could write as an old man: "I believe the future of the country to be of fairer promise than that of former years. And a higher sense of right and wrong, and a better land, are even now in sight."

The generation of Southerners who suffered, lost their all, and could feel that life held an even more glorious promise for the future, have left to their descendants a far more precious legacy than land or wealth.

Charles Spalding Wylly died in 1923 at the age of eighty-seven. He had never accepted charity, he owed no debts, and he left a sufficient sum to cover his last expenses. As he lay in his coffin he looked majestic clad in his old gray uniform, with the Confederate cross on his breast. His attendants were the representatives of the old families he had known and loved, of the Kings, Dents, Postells, Grants, Du Bignons, Nightengales, and Burroughs', while the pitiful old Confederate Veterans acted as an escort. He was taken by boat to Frederica, where he was met by all of the islanders, and as the sun set on Memorial Day he was laid to rest beside his wife in that beautiful run-down old cemetery, under the great oak trees and the drifting gray moss.

BIBLIOGRAPHY

BARTRAM, WILLIAM, *The Travels of William Bartram*
(1792–1794)

BOLTON, HERBERT E., *Spain's Title to Georgia* (1925)

BREMER, FREDERIKA, *Homes of the New World and
Impressions of America* (1853)

CATE, MARGARET DAVIS, *Our To-days and Yesterdays*
(1931)

CONRAD, GEORGIA BRYAN, *Reminiscences of a Southern
Woman* (1924)

Georgia Historical Collections (1840–1913)

Georgia Historical Quarterly (1917–1931)

HALL, BASIL, *Travels in North America* (1829)

HALL, MRS. BASIL, *The Aristocratic Journey* (1931)

HOWELLS, CLARK, *History of Georgia* (1926)

JONES, CHARLES C., JR., *History of Georgia* (1883)

KEMBLE, FRANCES ANNE, *Journal of a Residence on a
Georgia Plantation* (1863)

LEIGH, FRANCES BUTLER, *Ten Years on a Georgia
Plantation* (1883)

LYELL, SIR CHARLES, *Travels in North America*
(1849)

MURRAY, AMELIA M., *Letters from the United States,
Cuba and Canada* (1856)

SPALDING, THOMAS, *A Sketch of the Life of Oglethorpe* (1840)

STEVENS, REV. WILLIAM BACON, *Stevens History of Georgia* (1847)

WHITE, REV. GEORGE, *Historical Collections of Georgia* (1854)

WRIGHT, ROBERT, *A Memoir of General James Oglethorpe* (1867)

WYLLY, CHARLES SPALDING, *Memories; The Annals of Glynn; The Seed That Was Sown* (1910)

INDEX

INDEX

Butler, Fannie, daughter of Pierce, her account of James Hamilton Couper's funeral, 263, 264; her sympathy for the Southerners, 264; manages Georgia plantations, 267; married to Rev. James W. Leigh, 267.

Butler, Major Pierce, his property on St. Simon's Island, 72, 79–87; his career, 78, 79; his slaves, 79, 80, 85, 86, 106, 188, 189; entertains Aaron Burr, 82; moves to Philadelphia, 87; and Major Page, 95; his descent, 119; presents St. Clair house for Club House, 121, 122; entertains William Brailsford, 185.

Butler, Mrs., death, 86, 87.

Butler, Pierce (May), grandson of Major Pierce, marries Fanny Kemble, 196; his slaves, 198, 199, 200, 205, 211, 212; at James Hamilton Couper's funeral, 263; in the Civil War, 264; returns to Butler's Island, 265, 266; his account of death of Morris, 266; death, 267.

Butler, Mrs. Pierce. See Kemble, Frances Anne (Fanny).

Butler, Sarah, daughter of Pierce, her account of festivities at the Retreat, 251–253.

Butlers, of the old families, 127, 128, 193.

Butler's Island, 184, 196–200, 221, 251, 265.

Byrd, Mr., in the wreck of the *Pulaski*, 169, 177.

CABRERA, Governor of San Augustin, 15.

Calderon, Bishop of Cuba, 11.

Camden Hunt Club, 134–137.

Campana, Jean Baptist de, 12.

Cannon's Point, St. Simon's Island, granted to Capt. James McKay, 57; bought by John Couper, 72; description of, 72–78, 221; James Hamilton Couper at, 241–248; sold to Mr. Shadman, 270; house burned, 270; Charles Wylly quoted on, 270.

Carolina colonists, 14.

Carolinas, the, 18.

Caroline, Fort, 5.

Carolinians, slave labor used by, 28.

Carrs' Island, 231; taken for debt by Richard Corbin, 262.

Carteret's, 23.

Cat River, 22.

Cater, Annie, daughter of Benjamin, 231; married to John Postell, 269.

Cater, Benjamin Franklin, son of Thomas Cater, 92; at St. Clair Club dinner, 123; education of, 140; at Kelwyn Grove, 140; his family, 241.

Cater, Mrs. Benjamin, 241.

Cater, Thomas, 92.

Cavendish, Mr., 231, 232.

Chappeldelaine, M. de la, part owner of Sapelo, 97.

Charlefort, 5.

Charleston, 12, 14, 16.

Charlton, Thomas, at St. Clair Club dinner, 123, 124.

Châtelet (chocolate), property on Sapelo, 97, 110–116.

King, Floyd, in the Civil War, 259.

King, Florence, daughter of Thomas Butler, quoted, 146; married to Gen. Henry R. Jackson, 269.

King, Georgia, 209, 251, 253; her singing, 253, 254; married to Joseph J. Wilder, 269.

King, Hannah Lord, married to William Audley Couper, 250.

King, Henry Lord, in the Civil War, 259; death, 259; his grave, 259.

King, Mallory Page, son of Thomas Butler, 248; in the Civil War, 259; at the Retreat, 269.

King, Roswell, manager of Hampton Point estate, 87, 105.

King, Rufus, 181.

King, Thomas Butler, son of Daniel, Chairman of Naval Committee, 77; honorary member of Camden Hunt Club, 134; marries Anne Page, 145, 146; his character, 146; beloved by slaves, 146; public services of, 146, 248; his plantation, Retreat, 248–254; his family, 250; his fight for Southern rights before the Civil War, 258; sent by Governor Brown as Commissioner to Europe, 258; death, 259.

King, Mrs. Thomas Butler (Anne Page), 248–250; death, 258.

King, Thomas Butler, son of Thomas Butler, 249; death, 258.

King, Virginia, married to John Nesbit, 269.

LADSDEN, MR. of Charleston, given grant on St. Simon's Island, 58; sells Hampton Point tract, 72.

Lafil, Mr., 152.

Lamar, G. E., Mr. and Mrs. in the wreck of the *Pulaski*, 157.

Lanier, Sidney, quoted on St. Simon's Island, 129; poems of, inspired by Georgia coast, 272.

Lastere, Pedro de, 12.

Laurens, Gen. Henry, 65; Broughton granted to, 183.

Lawrence, St. Simon's Island, 88, 119.

Leake, Sarah, married to Thomas Spalding, 94, 107.

Legare, J. D., editor of *Southern Agriculturist*, quoted on Hopeton, 217.

Leigh, Canon James W., quoted on St. Simon's Island, 129; his religious work among the Negroes, 267.

Leigh, Lord, 267.

Leigh, Mrs., daughter of Mrs. Fanny Kemble Butler, 86, 210, 212.

Lincoln, Abraham, 260.

Little Brothers of Saint Francis. *See* Franciscans.

Little St. Simon's Island, 74.

Long Island, 78, 201, 221, 270, 275.

Long View, St. Simon's Island, 88.

Lord, Hannah, married to Daniel King, 146.

Lord, John, 139, 182, 244, 264.

besieged by Indians, 13.
See also St. Catherine's
Island.
Santa Elena, 5, 6, 8, 9.
Santa Maria, 11, 15.
Santa Maria de Guadeloupe,
Mission of, 17.
Santo Domingo de Telage,
Mission of, 8, 12.
Sapelo, 6, 17, 33; reserved by
Creeks as hunting island, 19;
deeded by Melatche to Mary
Musgrove, 60; ordered by
London Council to be sold
to highest bidder, 60;
ownership of, 97, 98; the
Châtelet, 97, 110–116; the
Spaldings, 98–110; social
life on, 110; hurricane at,
116–118; possessions of
Thomas Spalding on, 118,
236, 237; taken possession
of by runaway Negroes,
267; after the Civil War,
267–269; revisited, 273, 274.
Sapelo River, 26, 38, 66.
Savannah, founding of, 19;
citizens of, appeal for em-
ployment of slaves, 28; the
Wesleys at, 37, 39, 40.
Savannah River, 19, 23, 41.
Scots, in Georgia, 20–31; op-
posed to introduction of
slaves into Georgia, 29, 30.
Screven, Dr. of Savannah, 193.
Sea Island, 275. *See also*
Long Island.
Sedgwick, Elizabeth Dwight,
letters of Fanny Kemble to,
197, 198.
Shadman, Mr., buys Cannon's
Point, 270.
Shadman, William, son of Mr.
Shadman, 270.
Skidaway, 6.

Skidaway Scouts, 46.
Skye, Isle of, 21.
Slavery, banned from Colony
of Georgia, 18, 28, 29; petition against, 28–30; introduced into Georgia, 31, 60;
emancipation of, 271.
Slaves, their treatment and
characteristics, 99–104, 192–
194, 197–199, 202, 207–212,
218, 222, 223, 226–230, 249,
260, 265; their singing, 229,
230.
Small, Neptune, body servant
to Henry Lord King, 259.
Soldiers' Fort, St. Simon's
Island, 40, 41.
South Carolina, 42, 45, 47;
cedes claims to form Colony
of Georgia, 19.
South End home, Sapelo
Island, 104, 105, 109, 110,
116–118, 274.
South Newport River, 27.
Spain, claims of, on Atlantic
coast, 4, 18, 19, 40; at war
with England (1739), 42–
50; cedes Florida to Great
Britain, 62.
Spalding, Bourke, 237, 268.
Spalding, Captain Charles,
154.
Spalding, Elizabeth, married
to William Alexander
Wylly, 152, 153; goes to
Forest, 153, 154.
Spalding, James, partner of
Donald McKay, 64; marries
Margery McIntosh, 65;
buys Orange Hall, 65; birth
of son (Thomas), 65; en-
tertains Bartram, 67; re-
moves to Florida during
Revolution, 68; his return
after the Revolution, 70;

Spalding, James (*cont'd*)
death, 72, 94; his estate, 72, 249.
Spalding, John, 152.
Spalding, Matilda, 152.
Spalding, Randolph, in boat race, 247.
Spalding, Thomas, son of James, quoted, 25; birth, 65; admitted to bar, 94; marries Sarah Leake, 94; builds house for bride, 94; sells Orange Grove property to Major Page, 95, 96; in Scotland, 95, 96; returns to America, 96; moves to Sapelo, 97, 98; his slaves, 99, 100, 103, 104, 106; introduces sugar cane and the manufacture of sugar into Georgia, 100; his South End home, 104, 105, 116–118, 274; his library, 105, 268, 269; and Couper, 106–108; duties of the day on his plantation, 110, 111; importance of, 118; sent to Bermuda to negotiate with British, 118; helped frame constitution of Georgia, 118; character, 118; his Life of General Oglethorpe, 137; in later life, 236, 237; death, 237.
Spalding, Mrs. Thomas, 109; death, 236.
Spalding, Thomas, grandson of Thomas, 237; returns to Sapelo, 267, 268.
Spaniards, on Southern coast and islands of North America, 4–17; demand evacuation of territory south of St. Helena Sound, 40; attack Georgia coast, 44–46; repulsed from Fort William,

46; take Fort St. Simon's, 46, 47; repulsed at Frederica, 47; defeated at Bloody Marsh, 48, 49.
Stevens, John, 241.
Stevenses, the, 269.
Stiles, Robert Mackay, 231, 262.
Stowe, Harriet Beecher, her responsibility in the slavery matter, 271.
Stralbdean, Glen of, 21.
Stuart, Ensign, at Fort William, 46.
Sunbury, 61, 70; decline and disappearance of, 71.
Sunny South, 247.
Sutherland, Captain, in battle of Bloody Marsh, 48, 49.
Swarbreck, Captain, buys the Châtelet, 115.

TEACH, EDWARD ("Blackbeard"), pirate, 16.
Telaje, mission of Santo Domingo at, 12.
Timmons, Hannah, married to Major Page, 95.
Tolomato, Spanish outpost, 7, 10.
Tomocheche, Indian chief, 19, 32.
Toonahowie, Indian, 32.
Troup, Governor, 193, 194, 238.
Troup, Dr. James, at St. Clair Club dinner, 123, 126; his house, 154.
Tupiqui, Spanish outpost, 7, 11.
Turkeys, introduced into Europe, 9.
Twiggs, Duncan, 231.
Tybee Island, 6, 21.
USEEDA, JUAN DE, 12.

Van Renselaer, Julia, 253.
Velascola, Father, 10, 11.
Vernon, Edward, English Admiral, 45.
Village, the, St. Simon's Island, 55, 56, 88–90, 140, 240, 257, 270.
Virginia, 42.

Waddell, George, in Civil War, 256.
Walk-Away, 245.
Wambazee, Mr., 114, 115.
War of 1812, 143, 144.
Wardrobe, Lieutenant Colonel, 119.
Washington, George, and James McKay, 57, 58; at Valley Forge, 70; at Savannah, 70.
Wesley, Charles, and Oglethorpe, 37–39.
Wesley, John, in Georgia, 37, 39, 40.
West Point, St. Simon's Island, 88.
Whitfield, George, quoted, 50.
Whittaker, Miss, of Florida, married to Charles Wylly, 268.
Wilder, Joseph J., 269.
Wilder, Mrs. Joseph (Georgia King), visits Mrs Leigh, daughter of Fanny Kemble, 209, 211–213.
William, Fort, on Cumberland Island, 37; Spaniards repulsed at, 46.
Wilson, Janet, married to James Hamilton, 87.
Wister, Mrs. (Sarah Butler), 253.
Wood, Major, married to Elizabeth Brailsford, 185.
Wrights, the, 21.

Wylly, Capt. Alexander Campbell, 89, 90, 119, 120; at St. Clair Club dinner, 123, 125; his children, 140; his lines to Anne Page, 144.
Wylly, Mrs, Alexander Campbell, 89, 90, 140; description of, 239, 240; three spinster daughters of, 240.
Wylly, Alexander William, son of Alexander, 123, 127, 132, 140; marries Elizabeth Spalding, 152, 153; son born to, 154.
Wylly, Mrs. Alexander William (Elizabeth Spalding), son born to, 154.
Wylly, Anne, 152.
Wylly, Caroline Georgia, daughter of Alexander Campbell, 90; married to James Hamilton Couper, 147.
Wylly, Charles Spalding, son of Alexander William, 231; quoted, 60, 61, 89; his description of dinner at St. Clair Club, 122; how he called with his father at Major McIntosh's, 127, 128; birth, 154; his span of life, 155; on the days before and after Volstead, 192; on Christ Church, 203; on slavery, 209; his early life, 237, 238; his description of his grandmother, 239; on Cannon's Point, 242, 243, 270; a frequent visitor at Cannon's Point, 243; at boat race, 247; at the Retreat, 248; on Georgia King's singing, 253, 254; on the temper of the South in the Civil War, 255, 256; in the

Printed in the United States
114957LV00001B/58/A